A NEW
CATHOLIC
CATECHISM

A CENTER FOR MEDIA DEVELOPMENT, INC. BOOK

𝖘𝖉

STEIN AND DAY/*Publishers*/New York

A NEW

CATHOLIC

CATECHISM

BY FATHER PATRICK BERKERY

AND BROTHERS JOHN O'REILLY AND JOSEPH VALENTINE

Copyright © 1970 by Patrick Berkery, John O'Reilly and
    Joseph Valentine
Library of Congress Catalog Card Number 77-104638
All rights reserved
Published simultaneously in Canada by Saunders of Toronto, Ltd.
Designed by David Miller
Printed in the United States of America
Stein and Day/*Publishers*/7 East 48 Street, New York, N.Y. 10017
SBN 8128-1289-1

CONTENTS

INTRODUCTION

THE CATHOLIC CHURCH today is, to put it mildly, confusing. The papal encyclical reaffirming the traditional stand on birth control has caused deep unrest and honest questioning has met with pained reassertions of papal authority. Protesting clergy of the Archdiocese of Washington were defended in a national Catholic magazine. "Surely," the editor wrote, "a church as great and as resourceful as ours must know better ways to adjudicate a controversy than by almost daily announcements of suspensions and by locking priests out of their rectories." And he pleaded with American bishops "to use their influence to stop this disgraceful affair."

When Jacqueline Kennedy married a divorced man in an Eastern Orthodox ceremony, a respected cardinal said, "Why can't she marry whomever she wants to marry?" A noted official of the New York marriage court wrote in the Catholic magazine *America* that incompatible spouses caught in an "intolerable marriage" should be allowed to divorce and remarry. A Roman Catholic bishop, Francis Simons, has repudiated the biblical texts traditionally held up as proof of the existence of papal infallibility, thereby challenging one of the central doctrines of Catholicism; his book appeared at a time when Pope Paul was agonizing over the massive rebellion against his encyclical *Humanae vitae*. A priest columnist ridiculed the official prayers of the Church, calling some of them absurd and silly. Fifty-one priests from a Southern diocese accused their archbishop in a press conference of exercising authority in "an atmosphere of fear, alienation and dissatisfaction on the part of many priests."

The confusion is heightened by the contrast with the staid tranquility that once was the hallmark of doctrinal Catholicism. Similar rifts have occurred in the history of the Catholic Church, but what is unsettling—and new—is the inability of the leadership to control them or mitigate the increasing confusion and its subsequent tensions. Witness Bishop Helmsing of the Kansas City–St. Joseph diocese, who officially condemned the *National Catholic Reporter*, accusing the paper of "denying the most sacred values of our Catholic faith," calling the journal "poisonous" and "evil," and stating that he could not see how some of its writers could escape the penalty of automatic excommunication. The bishop was roundly put down by a lay editor of an Oklahoma diocesan newspaper, who considered the condemnation only the latest in a series of hard lines that make "it increasingly apparent that the leadership is scared half to death." He called the bishop's statement a historical aberration reflecting the mentality of the Inquisition. The bishops are to be pitied because of the painful depth of their fear, he added, and are to be resisted when they react with "medieval gobbledegook."

Where is it all going? How will it all end? The cry of the layman has become, "Thou art Peter, but who am I?"

In the "Declaration on the Relationship of Church to Non-Christian Religions" of Vatican II it is stated:

Men expect answers to the unsolved riddles of the human condition from religion. They are interested in finding out: (1) What is man? (2) What is the meaning of life? (3) What is moral good? (4) What is sin? (5) Whence suffering, what is its purpose? (6) What is the road to happiness? (7) What are death, judgment, and retribution after death? (8) Whence do we come and where are we going?

In the past Catholics had all these problems licked, because the Church considered itself the one, true, and only representative of Christ on earth, and the faithful loyally supported that thesis. The current wave of doubt, cynicism, and ferment sweeping through the Church is indeed of more than passing interest, especially to those Catholics who fail to see the emperor's new clothes.

Rebellion and revolution are not initiated by confused people. The leaders among the laity and the clergy are not confused. It is the ordinary person who is confused and who stands to be hurt most by what is happening in the bark of Peter. Why?

The majority of lay people do not read the specialized writings of the knowledgeable clergy and laymen. The circulation of the *National Catholic Reporter* is only 90,000 out of 50 million Catholics. Most Catholics know about the changes in the Church from the daily press. There they read of priests renouncing their vow of celibacy and marrying, about priests charging into churches and disrupting services, or pouring napalm on public property, or being sentenced to jail for civil disobedience. A television screen puts them face to face with men like ex-priest James Kavanaugh, author of *A Priest Looks at His Outdated Church,* and others who have deserted. They hear about people in Washington, D.C., walking out of church during Cardinal O'Boyle's sermon or about the elderly monsignor who fell to the floor of the sanctuary trying to prevent a priest from taking over another priest's pulpit. From this exposure, can the image of the leadership help but grow dimmer and dimmer?

The typical Catholic layman had a unique relationship with his Church and its leaders. He came to expect a certain style of direction and teaching. He knew his place. But he also was taught that when in doubt "Father knows best." So what must this layman feel now when a priest remarks that "the irreplaceable function of the priest . . . is precisely that of a cult leader, which is a one-hour-a-week job"?

Sunday after Sunday the priest had told the layman to follow the will of God, and taught him what to do to gain salvation, explaining the countless rituals and restraints that go along with being a Catholic. The priest taught him that eating meat on Friday was a sin and that he could be eternally damned for violating this law. Contraception was also a grave sin, as was missing Mass on Sunday. But now priests tell him otherwise. What condemned a man to hell yesterday doesn't seem to mean anything today. The layman cannot but gape as his leaders desert the ship once so zealously guarded. Is there something he doesn't know about? Who will clue him in? What's happening? As Frank Sheed wrote, "Is it the same Church?"

Rosemary Ruether remarks that the dilemma in Catholicism is that those awakened to a new vision of the Church are being turned off by the official bureaucracy and are drifting away without any new alternative emerging. Like James Kavanaugh, she is calling for a new type of Church. She claims that the liberals are getting tired of banging their heads against the stone wall of unmovable bureaucracy and are defecting. Underground churches are proliferating.

In both camps, liberal and conservative, there is a growing disenchantment with the existing Church leadership. And the ordinary layman is caught in the middle.

Confusion, undispelled by a fearful leadership, widens the gap between the layman and his once revered teachers. The layman is going off on his own, unaware of the consequences of his actions and unaided by those whose duty it is to provide him solace and encouragement. Robert E. Burns, executive editor of the *U.S. Catholic*, paints a true picture of the layman's attitude:

If it were possible for the American bishops to eavesdrop among American Catholic lay people, I'm sure they would be shocked to their shoes. Vast numbers of the "laity" care less and less about the things that preoccupy bishops and many pastors. Most of them retain their lifetime habit of attending Sunday Mass (thus obscuring their growing lack of interest) and not a few are temporarily lashed to the Church by their desire to send their children through parochial schools. But the old interest in the teachings of the Church, rekindled briefly during the excitement of Vatican II and the "changes" it brought, is ebbing seriously no matter what the bishops hear from the Knights of St. Gregory and Knights of Malta who have their ear. Drift is bad enough, but a turning away is worse. And it is obvious to anyone who is interested enough to look that Catholics are turning away in distaste and embarrassment as they witness a family quarrel growing more and more ugly in the street. (*Overview*, Nov. 1, 1968.)

Regardless of how one approaches the grave problems facing the Church, sooner or later he must relate the situation to himself. He, as a person, as a Catholic, is being dramatically influenced by the ferment in the Church. He can react by ceasing to be a Catholic, but he can only make such a decision in terms of what he has to lose, psychologically and socially. He must be prepared to accept the risks of such withdrawal.

Or he can stay and help rebuild, for the key to positive renewal is the layman himself; the leaders are afraid. If he chooses to remain, he cannot continue in his former stance, that of mute lamb to powerful shepherd. The shepherds are not the same. They are no longer equipped to save their flocks, judging by their performance in present crises.

The layman, then, stands to lose the most should the Church collapse. He must act and take on a leadership role, simply because it is now a question of his own survival. He has to make a decision, one that he must live with and one that if left unmade could destroy him. Fortunately, Vatican II has outlined for him a rich, fertile source of power over his own religious destiny. His is a new role within a renewed Church, one supported by the decree on *The Church in the Modern World.*

Before the layman can move into a new position within the Church, he must first decide whether or not he is willing to abide by his commitment to a previous concept of the Church. Once he has settled this basic option, then he must assume his new status and his new obligations. But this is possible only if he understands the changes that have swept through the Church and is able to gauge the effect these changes have on his own personal life and destiny. Only then can he accept the intense responsibility.

First, the layman must prepare himself. In the past few years a deluge of information on the changes in the Church has appeared in the popular press. Thus most people are aware of significant changes. Despite all the publicity given such issues as clerical celibacy, birth control, and Friday abstinence from meat, many people do not comprehend the long-range effects such drastic changes imply.

The climate of change is punctuated and indeed nourished by the myriad books explaining the "new Church." One reviewer wrote that he was bored to death with the vultures that hover over the Church in its throes. All have the same message—and it is sheer drama.

If the layman intends to be an effective instrument of change, he must do his homework. Or even if he decides to walk away from the Church, he must know why he does so. Although he cannot be expected to read everything that has been written since Vatican II, the layman needs some direction to help him see the total picture. He should review what he once believed, or at least what was once considered valid doctrine, and from this solid base he should study the alternatives currently being presented, discussing, criticizing, seeking out more information about them.

The manner in which this investigation is made is quite important. The German philosopher Hegel is responsible for an intellectual device that has proven of immense value in the development of concept formations. This is the Hegelian triad, whereby a thesis is proposed and its opposite is immediately positioned into conflict with it. Hegel taught that from such a confrontation of opposites a balanced third view, known as synthesis, can be developed. Far from being a parlor game, this exercise in creativity has sparked many contemporary theories. The use of the Hegelian triad moves discussion away from the infantile bickering of conservative versus liberal and toward a tangible goal. The discussant may end up switching from an either/or to a both/and attitude.

In writing this book, we have accepted the reality of change. We have not sought to offer explanations or apologies for the extent and pace of the changes. As clergymen, we understand the position of the institutional Church, and we can sympathize with the leadership, without condoning its ostrich-like posture. Change always brings vexing problems, but we cannot ignore the fact that the present violent upheaval stems in large part from the Church's unwillingness to accept change. Had the changes been prepared for through planned reorganization, the result might have been less tumultuous.

What is now needed is a reconsideration of some basic issues from both the new and old perspectives. We shall try to present a fair picture of each issue, avoiding caricature but allowing anomalies to reveal themselves. The traditional viewpoint presented here may at times seem a caricature to some readers, but this material has come, often verbatim, from such treasured handbooks as the *Baltimore Catechism* and even the "Question Box." The few liberal views may horrify some people. We do not employ shock for its sake alone, but to induce constructive reflection. We did not initiate the changes described in this book. We are merely trying to capture the essence of two worlds—two worlds that must either co-exist for some time or destroy one another.

We want to drive home one point, which is simply that the consequences of change must be met. Unless Catholics reconcile themselves to the shape of things to come, their religious world is disaster-destined. Salvation is no longer a point in the future; it is part of the now.

To move intelligently and creatively within a changing world, a man must be a step ahead of change. He does this by searching to understand the causes behind the changes and by relating the change process to his own life, to his own needs, psychological and otherwise. A sound method of diagnosing the forces beneath the current is analysis born of comparison, whereby one matches the old with the new. In this way a synthesis with which one can live emerges. Reaction diminishes, and controlled direction takes over.

Why shouldn't we discuss the transformation of a once high and haughty Church? People are generally loath to talk about religion unless threatened. We submit that imposed, incomprehensible change can destroy in one blow a lifetime of habits, traditions, and beliefs. This is a more insidious threat. How threatened a reader feels depends on how great is his need for fortresses, cabbages, and kings.

Spirited dialogue can ventilate the mustiness of centuries. Good healthy confrontation between the old and the new might blow away unhealthy fears and return the self to self. Who knows?

This book encourages positive action. We are convinced that in an area so vital and penetrating as religion, change must not destroy, but rebuild and revitalize. Religion will be saved by people who can read the signs of the times and, with that knowledge, move forward, understanding the forces dictating change and thus able to come to grips with them.

In other words, we feel religion must return to the people. We sympathize with the multitude of supermarket Catholics who, once wont to shop in church once every Sunday to be nourished on frozen, instant religion, are now bewildered that the once heavily laden shelves are bare.

If we come across as iconoclastic, it's because religion has been so much hidebound ritual, and that strikes us as wrong and upside down. Religion is life. Christ came that we might have life and have it abundantly. Life means action. It demands getting in there and helping others to live more fully, showing them how to get their share of it all.

Are we idealists? Or are we realists?

We opt for realism. A realist has windows; an idealist, mirrors. A realist picks up clay and fashions a man. An idealist picks up clay and washes his hands.

We hope the reader's response will not be passive. Whether you are irritated by what we say or not, we hope that at least you'll talk, discuss, argue. Perhaps you'll want to do something positive about the changes presently being opted for within the Church. At the very least, you'll know that if the new religion upsets you, you are not completely without fault, for the thrust of that "new religion" depends on you more than you might realize. A free exercise of religion is one of the highest values of the human spirit. To turn your back on that exercise is to espouse ultimate disaster.

In his book Father James Kavanaugh said the Church was "outdated." He was helpful, since he popularized many new currents within the Church and forced many people to rethink their positions. But then he left and took himself a wife. He was a man who shot and ran. He preferred not to remain to help build up what he called a dying institution. He struck out.

A *New Catholic Catechism*, however, tries to suggest a blueprint for positive action. We want the layman to help rebuild the Church.

Some have told us that this is a dangerous book, because it is not authorized by the Church; that it spreads confusion because most lay people are not sophisticated enough to distinguish opinion from fact or theological theory from revealed truth; that great harm can result from do-gooders and cynical critics of institutional religion. For what else can emerge when frenzied messianic prophets take it upon themselves to dispense their own brand of truth and in-thinking? The proper source for clarification and mass education, these critics conclude, is Rome or the diocesan chancery office.

We feel that this book is far from dangerous. Dangerous to whom? The layman? In these pages, he is at least offered an opportunity to make up his own mind, for he is presented with as objective an explanation as possible.

A *New Catholic Catechism* is an attempt to fill a leadership void, to serve as a stimulus to the clergy and the hierarchy. It presents no threat but truth. The clerical mind is sometimes unable to understand that the world has changed drastically since medieval times. In a free society, to suppress or withhold the truth is almost impossible. The truth refuses to remain hidden; it is this fact that is behind so much of the ferment and anxiety in the Church today.

This book provides comprehensive information unavailable elsewhere in any single source. The average layman has been kept in the dark too long about things that pertain to his life and his values.

Diogenes said that "the only good is knowledge and the only evil is ignorance." We are endeavoring to stand on the side of knowledge. We believe that one of the greatest evils in the modern Church is the information gap.

We cannot conclude that the book ought not to have been written because some readers might be shocked or disillusioned by it. Such an attitude implies that the average layman is not capable of wrestling with the truth and that he is not intellectually equipped to grasp the very truth affecting his destiny.

We reject such a thesis as pernicious and defeating. For any layman to cower behind the protective and closed attitude so reflected is to espouse living death.

Properly used, this book can achieve much good. For one thing, it might help the layman realize how restraining is the ecclesiastical umbilical cord that controls his mind's nourishment and his soul's direction.

We do not offer this book as an end in itself. It makes no claim to scholarship, or to completeness, but it does deal with the basic, the significant, the central. We propose its method as a stimulus to further thought and eventual action. We would like to think it leads to a beginning.

I

THE PERSON

WHY DID GOD make you? Remember the *Baltimore Catechism?* It says: "God made me to know him, to love him, to serve him in this world and to be happy forever with him in the next."

The Catholic religion has always taught that existence is God-oriented. The Creator dictates your reason for being. Christ made the Catholic Church his official and sole voice in the world. The Church alone can tell you what God wants and how he would like to be served.

When you were a child, you became a member of the Catholic Church through the rite of baptism. In return for your soul, the Church promised to show you how to live on earth and prepare for heaven.

What does the Catholic Church think about you? First of all, it says you are composed of a body and a soul. Your soul is more important to the Church than your body. The desires of the body, its emotions, get in the way of the soul. They are genuine obstacles to knowing, loving, and serving God.

At a tender age the Church, through the nuns and priests, explained the mortal sin of your first parents, Adam and Eve. You learned that this original sin affected you and everyone else in the world, but that the Church was empowered to erase the sin through the sacrament of baptism.

As a human being living under the aegis of the Catholic Church, your main preoccupation is to save your soul. You can be saved only if you avoid sin, and strive to be perfect.

The Church teaches that you are imperfect. God is perfect, man is not. But through faithful observance of the rules and regulations of your religion, you can become closer to perfection. As a Catholic, you spend your life trying to become perfect like God, and you have a measure of success to the extent that you keep your soul pure. If you fail to obey the Church you can commit a mortal sin. In the event of sudden death, the consequences of this sin would be eternal hell.

The Church is empowered to offer forgiveness if you humbly admit your guilt. In the confessional you can discover whether or not your actions were merely a slight offense against the law of God.

A good Catholic strives to be "childlike" in his approach to God. But though he follows all the Church's rules, in the end he can be damned. Grace, or the life of the soul, is not something one can count on. Paradoxically, a person can ignore the Church and on his deathbed still be saved.

Catholicism forces you to be heavily dependent upon the Church. "I am a Catholic. In case of accident, call for a priest." As long as the priest is at your side when death strikes, eternal bliss is yours.

Childlike dependency can be very comforting, but since the changes resulting from Vatican II you have been given more responsibility. To understand the changing Church and your place in it you must re-examine the following basic questions.

1. DO YOU KNOW WHO YOU ARE?

§   YES

"Know thyself," say the ancient philosophers, and this is sound advice. Most psychologists bemoan the fact that many people do not know who they really are. They have Walter Mitty–type dreams and set goals for themselves that are not only unrealistic but often harmful. A good Catholic knows who he is, because he finds his understanding of self in his belief in God. We are made to the image and likeness of God. We come from God and are on our way to God.

I know myself as a human being, complete with imperfections and destructive tendencies. I know myself as a weak person constantly in need of direction and discipline so that I may not betray the trust that God has given me. I do not know myself completely because I do not know God completely, but I have enough knowledge of myself to be aware of my limitations and my resources. I have a distinctive personality and a specific awareness of myself that no one else can have. I pray to God daily to help me overcome my faults with his grace and his blessings.

We are told that a just man falls seven times daily, and with that knowledge I know that it will be difficult keeping myself in the state of grace. I turn to the sacraments frequently and try to keep out of mortal sin. Because of original sin and the innate weakness of human nature this task will be even harder. But with all the help that the Church gives me I am not afraid. If God is with me, who can be against me. I don't expect to do exceptionally great things, but I try to live my life in such a way that when Judgment Day comes God will see me as one who knew his own limitations and, despite them all, tried his best to remain faithful to the laws of the Church.

Those people who are always searching for their identity are perplexing individuals. We are what we are and cannot change. Knowledge is coupled with faith, and without my religion I would feel inadequate. I define myself in relation to my religion, and I find consolation in the fact that I am a Catholic. It gives me strength to move ahead and try to make some contribution to a world in dread and torment. People who give up their faith simply because of an injustice or a misunderstanding with Church authorities do not understand the importance of the Church. St. Augustine said that the human heart is restless until it rests in God.

Our world today needs men of courage and vision, but they must understand the traditions of our forefathers to be able to move in the direction of God. The Christians who braved the lions and the torture racks because they believed in Christ knew who they were and so knew what was expected of them. In their close relationship to God and the Church they received the power of God, a power that made mere mortal life so inconsequential when compared to immortality and heaven.

✶ NO

I am not quite sure who I am. I know who I am supposed to be and also what I would like to be. But were I to say that I really know who I am, I would be untrue to myself. I am not undergoing an identity crisis. Rather I am withholding knowledge of myself so that I may know myself even more perfectly. I do not know myself to emphasize that I want to be myself. The pious clichés that tell me I am a child of God or that I am a soldier of Christ are meaningless.

First of all, definitions are dangerous because they can limit potential. I like to think of myself as unique, as something special, but I don't define myself. Just when I think I know myself, I change. I'm not the same person I was yesterday, and that thought, far from being frightening, is thrilling. If someone else defines me, I would like to know the categories he is using and by what right he puts labels on people.

A person says that he is a Christian; I would like to know what a Christian is. No person can really be defined in an abstract manner because every person is different. A Christian in Egypt is not the same as a Christian in Uruguay. A human being naturally resists definition, especially in relationship to another. For example, to say that one is made in the image and likeness of God is one thing, but to force a person to direct his life in accordance with so abstract a concept is definitely unfair and inhuman. No man has seen God, so no man can say what God is like.

I like to consider myself as an unknown quantity. In that way, I go about giving form and shape to myself each day. I am like a sculptor. I hammer and I chisel this way and that. If I don't like the result of my labors, then I change. Maybe I stress this or maybe I eliminate that. I do things because I feel that they are right and because I am free. Definition takes away my freedom. If the definition is imposed by a cult or a culture, then it forces me to live up to something that is from outside myself and therefore is an intrusion on my pattern of action.

I am not a dreamer, nor am I unrealistic. I realize that many influences act upon me, striving to force me in one direction rather than another. But I am free to select or reject. That is what makes me different from an animal. I have my own mind, and I make my own judgments based upon the evidence presented to me. Not that I reject history and the experience of others. Rather, life for me is something that I experience, that I plunge into. With that in mind, I am open to change and open to revitalization. In the morning I awaken and am happy to be alive. I enter into experience and find myself different at the end of each day because of my willingness to take risks and to encounter new forces. I think what changes me most is meeting another person with similar openness and courage. Such a person acts on me and leaves his imprint on my personality.

Do not think I am frivolous because I don't know who I am. With this approach to life, I can look forward to excitement and to enterprise. I can grow and mature because I have not set any limits or ceilings. I can bounce back from life's blows. I enjoy life and people. I have so much to look forward to and so many things I want to do. I try almost everything because only through experience can I know what is good for me and what is harmful. I am not playing games, nor am I a stereotyped individual. I play no roles, and I am not someone else. I am who I am, and that is enough for me. A label, a small box to put myself in, these do not interest me. What did God say when they asked him who he was? "I am who I am." What did Jesus say?

2. DO YOU THINK THE BODY IS DETRIMENTAL TO THE SOUL?

§ YES

Unfortunately, on most occasions the body does not seek the best interests of the soul. The body seeks its own comfort. After all, the body has neither intelligence nor will; it is sheer matter.

The soul, on the other hand, is spiritual. The soul knows and it wills. The soul is the seat of humanity. The body is animalistic.

All the body's desires and lusts drag me away from God. When Sunday comes it is my body that makes me lazy and keeps me from fulfilling my obligation to attend Mass. Impure thoughts and desires arise from the flesh. The body is the seat of sins like gluttony, lust, envy, and sloth.

The Church teaches that in the resurrection on the final day, the body will rise glorious and immortal, cleansed of its evil tendencies.

But now the body is my cross. It is imperfect and will not be perfect until that final day. It is, as St. Francis of Assisi called it, "my brother ass."

✳ NO

The body and soul are dual forces operating in one being. I reject the contrived opposition between body and soul; it turns one into a self-hater.

God created the body and is, I'm sure, proud of his handiwork. Man is created as a whole in the image and likeness of God. When we deprecate our body, we insult God.

From the findings of modern psychology and science, we discover the importance of the mutual relationship of body and soul. Even Thomistic philosophy refers to both as principles of life, each making a distinctive contribution to the totality of man.

God showed his pride in his creation of man when he came down to earth as a flesh-and-blood being—Christ did not walk the earth as a disembodied spirit.

Too many Catholics make the body a scapegoat for their failings. They become split personalities. And they ignore the potential of a healthy body-image.

I like to look upon my soul as a power of the body, rather than its enemy. In this way, I approach life realistically. I confidently meet my responsibilities.

3. IS LIFE A PLAN
   RATHER THAN A PROMISE?

§ YES

Life must be planned, for God gave us only one life. Are not good business practices the result of a good plan? So, too, life itself demands organization and planning to achieve its goals.

To reject planning in life is to spend one's time in wishful thinking. In his arguments for the existence of God, St. Thomas showed that nature itself reflects plan and design.

Design and structure flow from the need for specific goals. When you are going to have a party, you have to plan a menu and so on. If you want to build a house, you need a blueprint. And so the greatest venture of all, life itself, must be planned.

Life is too precious a gift to waste. One cannot believe that God gave us the gift of life to squander it aimlessly. Life has purpose, and whenever you have purpose you need planning.

This is where the Catholic Church comes in. The Church helps us plan our day-to-day God-centered activity. This is what spirituality and asceticism are all about.

Anyone believing that life is more promise than plan deludes himself. He shirks responsibility and doesn't face up to life. He can never achieve anything because everything is left to chance. And saddest of all, he abandons his destiny.

The hippies are examples of people living without plan. They reject the Church and its helpful guideposts and end up desperate, dreaming away existence. Ultimately, they must turn to something for an escape—drugs, séances, occult sciences, or something far worse.

✳ NO

There is no real opposition between planning and promise. He who would reject any life vision as a promise is foolish. He reneges on a basic responsibility. It is easier to let other people do the planning and tell you how to live.

In reality no one can escape the burden of life's promise. When one looks on life as a promise, he becomes more optimistic and committed to life.

Life is not a set of rules, but a challenge. That challenge is uniquely personal and cannot be exchanged for another's. This dimension of personal responsibility toward life sometimes escapes those who would eagerly accept other people's designs for their lives. Planned living becomes lackluster and drab, whereas creativity, challenge, and opportunity leap out of a life that sees itself as fulfillment of promise rather than leaden, programmed servility.

Life cannot be lived in a vacuum. Neither can it be lived in an objective, depersonalized manner. Contemporary man best illustrates this point. One who postulates plan over promise overlooks the fact that, through his creative insights, the successful businessman is one who breaks out of conformity and achieves.

Promise, then, is not undisciplined, but it is freeing and exhilarating. Promise does not defy nature. It reflects that very spirit differentiating man from beast.

In fulfilling the promise of his own personal life, based on his insights and his understanding, man best achieves the maximum use of his freedom.

4. DO YOU LIKE RELATING TO GOD AS A CHILD?

§ *YES*

God is my Father, and the Catholic Church is my mother. I am their child, and without their help I would be all alone.

Christ told us to be "as little children." His love of children is shown throughout the Gospels, and he himself was pure and childlike. I am a Christian if I follow his example: a combination of mature love and childlike humility.

The layman must have a childlike relationship to the Church, for the Church knows so much more than he. It has the experience of centuries and the promise of Christ, who said he would be with it all days, even unto the consummation of the world. The good Catholic depends on the Church. It gives him his spiritual food. It directs his actions and chastises him when he goes astray.

I cannot conceive of any other way to relate to the Church than as a child. People who would rebel against the Church reveal protracted adolescence.

The Church has given everyone so much, for it is the representative of God on earth. He who hears the Church hears God. In the Eucharist especially there is comfort and solace.

St. Theresa was a perfect example of how effective a childlike attitude toward God and the Church can be. The way of Theresa is the perfect way, for she showed that true happiness is

found within the religious family, each of us a faithful and devoted child of the mother Church and God the Father.

✳ NO

If I am a child, I will relate to God as a child. But if I am
an adult, I will not act as a child, nor will I accept being treated
as one.

The Catholic Church in the past has been too literal in calling us its "children." I am an adult. I relate to God from and
through my actual life situation.

Christ treated his apostles and followers as men. He con-
fided the establishing of his Church to adults, not to children.
The Pope does not consider himself a child, nor do bishops and
priests.

It is to the advantage of the bishops and priests to force a
childlike humility upon the laity. Children can be ignored. Children can be sent to bed without supper if they misbehave.

I relate to God as an adult. If the Church is to be a genuine
go-between for myself and God, then the Church has to accept
me as I am. I do not expect to be deferred to, but I insist that
I be heard on equal terms, not as a child.

I think the insistence of the Church on childlike qualities
turns religion into an Alice in Wonderland kind of game. It also
affords Church officials a diabolical instrument of control and
deception. Authoritarian parents do not condescend to explain
their actions to a child.

5. DO YOU KNOW WHAT YOU HAVE TO LOOK FORWARD TO?

§ YES

I look forward to a life filled with challenge and peace. Peace
is the awareness that I am doing God's will and fulfilling his law.
Order is achieved when a human being acts like a human being
and so fulfills his nature. There is much uncertainty to life be-

cause no one knows when he is going to die. We have little control over future events. Each person must live in the present. A good Catholic not only lives in the present, he lives in the presence of God.

Many of the great saints feared nothing of the future, and dread of it held no power over their lives. They acquired this tranquil attitude by invoking God's presence. They saw God everywhere, but primarily in their hearts, for they were pure and holy in the sight of the Lord.

Contact with God is so important and so vital to inner peace. It is natural to worry about the future. The young especially feel they must act to direct it. It takes an almost saintly resignation to overcome this concern—particularly in the twentieth century —but we must strive to achieve it. Things will happen that we do not like, but life is not a bed of roses. If, however, one is resigned to the will of God, no evil can really befall him.

Christ tells us in the Gospels to fear those who can kill the soul rather than those who can harm the body. Sin kills the soul and makes us unpleasing in the sight of God, but what person can force us to sin? Few indeed.

Many good people lie in hospital beds with painful and serious illnesses, but they manage to smile although they know they have little to look forward to. They are happy and at peace, for they are like the suffering Christ, who knew that his future on earth would be rejection and painful death.

A priest once told me, "It's not what happens to you in life that is important. Rather it's how you react." Although I know that all there is to look forward to in this life is uncertainty, this knowledge can be accepted with resignation and peace. The providence of God sustains each of us and keeps us moving forward.

There is a great movement today in the Church that emphasizes the theology of hope. My hope is my confidence in God and my willingness to abide by his will. In the seventeenth century many people misinterpreted the concept of divine providence and became quietists. They did not accept any obligation to do good, but simply sat on the riverbanks and passively awaited the coming of the Lord. Even St. Paul had his hands filled with those who thought Christ's second coming was so imminent that they could not afford to go out and get involved in the business of charity and Church.

By keeping busy with the things that pertain to God and religion, I am able at the same time to develop a serenity and a spirit of abandonment to the will of God. Fate and chance do not frighten me, since I fail to see their place in a universe designed and structured for a specific goal by an almighty Creator. What is the future and what does it hold for me? I know and I don't know, yet I know the peace of doing the will of God.

❋ NO

I don't know what I have to look forward to, but I live my life from day to day with a good understanding of what life is all about. The Catholic religion tells us that we must live under the providence of God. This concept can lead to abuses if pushed too far. God is made the scapegoat for too many of our mistakes. Not worrying about the future leaves me free to worry about today. And this is what is most important: to concentrate on the present moment for the right motivation, and not cast off fear of tomorrow by aligning oneself with nebulous goals and fanciful theories. The impulse of man's life is within himself, and the conduct of that life is his responsibility. We blame God for too many things, so to escape the blame of our own ineptitude.

I think my future will be largely of my own making. By that I mean that whatever happens tomorrow has its roots in today. The future really will be my own creation. God gave me the vision, the opportunity, and the promise. It remains to me to ensure the proper development of my future.

I see the theology of hope as vague speculation. It is helpful to a degree, but when theory forces me to concentrate too deeply on how my tomorrow can take a peaceful turn rather than a painful twist, then I resent this theology as interference. I make my own tomorrows and I am responsible for them. To make today happy, some say I should think about what God can give me tomorrow. When do I get down to the business of fulfilling the present so that it can burst into a new tomorrow?

I like to think of the resurrection of Christ and how one day I too will rise toward eternal fulfillment. But I cannot afford to make this dream an excuse for inactivity, and especially for rejection of today. The business of life for me is not an odious or fearful obligation. Life is a constant, moving and dynamic. I act and am acted upon, and I can stand apart from myself in deep reflection to catch the movement of life. But I never lose hold of the reins. I see God's influence in the opportunity and incentive he affords me. But I never ask him to do what I am supposed to do. I never relate to him as if he had given me nothing and kept all to himself. I see him about me and I know he is there. But he stands apart from me; he does not act for me or dictate to me, but simply inspires and encourages me. God expects me to use my talents and to offer him the fruits of my endeavors.

This firm control over my life is what makes me confident in facing the future. I think this is what God expects of us— that we be in control and that we produce from the power of his gifts. My hope is in myself because I trust what God has done for me in his creation, his gift of the world to me. My hope is limitless because God's goodness has been lavish.

I don't look to the future. I am too busy with the present. Vatican II released man from a false bondage to the future by revealing the beauty and power of the individual. Resourcefulness and dynamism are the gifts of God to man. We have little to gain from hoarding our potential and deluding ourselves through baseless hope into believing that God will keep us from harm and danger. Confidence in man is the greatest tribute we can pay to God in return for fashioning us and providing us with priceless opportunities.

6. DO YOU BELIEVE IN THE INTELLECT, WILL, AND EMOTIONS?

§ YES

The intellect is that power in the human being which enables him to think. It is through the intellect that man is able to assimilate things outside himself and make them part of his own world. Intellect is a powerful force in man and unless it is understood as a spiritual power, it makes little sense.

Many scientists maintain that man's intellect is situated in his brain and that it is a material substance which can be formed and controlled. Some scientists maintain that animals have an intellect, since all intellect is simply an ability to solve problems. Because animals are able to overcome obstacles and difficulties, they conclude, animals therefore have intellects.

For me the intellect is a spiritual faculty within the human soul. It is spiritual because man's soul is spiritual. As a result of original sin man's intellect was impaired, and he is not able to comprehend as capably as he should. He does not see things in their proper light, and often his judgment is incorrect. The intellect is able to perceive truth, but because of original sin it is often blinded to reality and seeks its own selfish ends.

As important as the intellect is man's will, which is that power through which man is able to seek after good. Goodness is the object of man's will, but because of his impaired intellect he is not always able to achieve absolute goodness. Through the will man is able to make a free choice, which cannot be tampered with or regulated by forces outside himself. For this reason, it is important for man to understand the things he seeks and to seek only those that are good for his eternal salvation.

The intellect and the will are man's highest faculties. Through the first he can obtain truth and through the second, goodness.

The emotions are secondary in man's psychological makeup, but they are important, because they must be reckoned with. But for a man to allow his emotions to run his life is to live as an animal. These are powers that man has in common with the animals, and their function is essential: they provide him with some direct contact with his environment. If he were deprived of his emotions and his sense faculties, he would be imprisoned within himself. This was proved in the case of Helen Keller, who without the patient and skilled instruction of her mentor could never have overcome blindness and deafness and achieved the intellectual brilliance that crowned her life.

Emotions tend to drag us down instead of lifting us up toward the spiritual. Emotions can color our judgments and distort our appreciation of goodness; they can be both helpful and harmful. Prayer, mortification, and keen discipline are needed to strike a balance.

✳ *NO*

Man is a thinking animal, and he has appetites. Any deprecation of man's emotional self is objectionable to me. I prefer to think of Pope John's definition of man, used in his encyclical *Peace on Earth*, as a being possessing intelligence and freedom rather than intellect and will.

When I think of man as an intelligent being, I also think of him as creative and resourceful, and of his potential contribution as a person. The object of man's intelligence is the world about him. Man uses his intelligence to achieve a harmony between himself and his environment.

The view that intellect is intelligence obviates any need to distinguish between the material and the spiritual, for intellect is then viewed as an interrelational dynamic rather than as a complex, disembodied movement beyond man. Truth becomes something tangible and thus loses its mystical absoluteness. Even St. Thomas, with all his abstract explanations of the psychological within man, maintained that truth is a relationship or a conformity between man and his world. When we concentrate on man's abstract powers, we begin to lose sight of the beauty of truth and its closeness to the human spirit. We conceive of truth as an unachievable absolute, and then we set up guardians of truth who try to foist upon man an understanding of truth that is basically inhuman, because it is unreal.

Intelligence is closely linked with freedom and, for me, freedom is always intelligent and responsible. One philosopher ridiculed the concept of free will because he could not put his finger on a will within man. But the exercise of free will is what makes freedom tangible and comprehensible. Those who suppress freedom fail to see that the instinct to freedom flows from intelligence. Without intelligence there is no freedom.

Within the Church freedom has been a rare commodity because the Church did the thinking for the faithful. Few people realized that once they allowed the Church to tamper with their intelligence they had to accept the consequences, namely, that they were no longer free to act as human beings. To my way of thinking, only human beings are capable of acting with freedom, and a person who allows his freedom to be usurped demeans himself.

The emotions are friends of intelligence and freedom. The emotions have received a short shrift from the Church because they supposedly interfere with the spiritual life. But hate, love, fear, anguish, are human powers and as such they form an important part of the human constellation. To call them secondary in man's nature is not necessarily to equate them with inferiority, but this has been a mistake in the Church's psychological understanding of man. As a result, man has suppressed his emotions and waged war within himself instead of using the unique power that can be his through an integrated spiritual and emotional life.

Modern psychology has advanced our knowledge of man through analysis of his emotions. We have seen what can happen when man completely suppresses his emotions. He can become sterile, dogmatic—and even totalitarian in his approach to life and to interpersonal relationships. Psychologists counsel clients to release their emotions, to let themselves go and to be themselves. This I think is the key to stable and sound understanding of self: Be yourself. Accept yourself with your limitations and with your powers and then go out and live.

Christ cried, he became angry, he laughed, he consoled those who were in sorrow. He was truly human because he accepted himself. He was free, he was intelligent, and he was emotional.

It is important to understand our powers and the natural interrelationship between them established by the Creator. This I believe to be the obligation of all men, namely, that each understand and utilize the fantastic endowment given him as a human being. Then let him go forth and be human!

7. DO YOU ACCEPT THE TRADITIONAL EXPLANATION OF FREE WILL?

§   *YES*

Free will is the capability of determining what is good for me as an individual. It is basically self-determination. It is a kind of property or power that I, as a rational being, can either use or withhold. Free will, then, is an exercise of choice.

The concept of free will is embodied in the moral consciousness of mankind. This sense of moral obligation is found in the heart of every man. That man has a free will is as certain as the laws of nature. Just as we know that trees grow straight up, that clouds hover above us, and that birds make nests, so too can we be sure from our own awareness of ourselves that we have a free will.

We know also that as responsible human beings we strive to act rightly and refrain from acting wrongly. We know that we are absolutely free to avoid moral evil. The determinist insists that we do the things we do precisely because we have to. On the contrary, we act as we do because we want to. We can commit an evil act, but then we lose our freedom. We are free to turn ourselves into non-free beings. Evil causes us to be non-free because evil is opposed to good, and thus cannot logically be the object of our will. Even when we perform an evil act, we are proving the fact that we have a free will.

Catholics have been taught that whatever good they perform will be rewarded in heaven. God will punish evil and reward good. When a person acts in a God-like manner, filled with charity and love, when he fulfills the law of God and obeys the laws of the Church, then he can say that he is meriting God's favor and an increase in glory in heaven. The very concept of merit presupposes free will. If I avoid temptation or make a painful sacrifice, then I feel that I should receive some kind of reward. But if I am *forced* to do good, then what reward is owed me?

Those who deny the freedom of the will are called 'determinists or fatalists. Theirs is a gloomy, pessimistic approach to life, destructive of religion and goodness. Defining man as a mere robot and a slave to his environment does nothing to enhance the dignity of mankind or the graciousness of our Father in heaven. In fact, determinism denies the essential notion of responsibility, and makes us mere pawns in the hands of a cruel and sadistic God.

Free will is true freedom. A definition attributed to Bishop Sheen states that "freedom is the right to do what we ought." But the fact that our will is limited by goodness and responsibility in no way denies the reality that we are constantly free to act or not act. God does not force us to love him. We are free to accept Christ or reject him, but we must also know that we are responsible for the consequences of our actions; we must consider what the rejection of Christ would imply in terms of eternity.

❈ NO

I reject the traditional explanation of free will simply because it does not take the total man into consideration. Moreover, one usually ends up "choosing freely" because of fear of damnation. In other words, the Church teaches that you have a free will, but that you'd better do such-and-such or else you'll burn forever. I think more of freedom than of free will, because freedom is real and is exercised. Free will is simply a term, a name, nothing more. The concept of free will encourages men to run away from themselves into a safe, dark corner, waiting for instructions from on high.

Human freedom involves the whole person. Man has power and direction, he determines his own fate.

Sartre considers freedom ultimately absurd, but he and the other existentialists have a better understanding of man than did the Scholastics. The existential concept of freedom is more realistic and open: man exists and is born to be free—to be open to change and growth. By being, we are free. If we view freedom as intimately bound to man's existence, then there should be no need to guarantee it by a web of legislation. But freedom is calling for more existence and more power.

What man is really using his freedom when he stifles himself or his neighbor? What man is truly growing and remaining open to life if he stifles the call for involvement and concern? The key to the understanding of freedom is found in the very promise of life itself. And the person living life to its fullest is one who moves freely within the world.

Freedom is not only independence, or power to control one's own destiny; it cannot exist in isolation. Freedom is humanity, it is caring and tenderness; freedom is love in action and a contributor to the totality of mankind. Freedom is a gift of God, for, as St. Paul says, we are not slaves but are free with the freedom of the children of God. Freedom is so intimately bound up with self-knowledge and -awareness that one can easily discern those who know themselves by how they use the gift of freedom. Fear and hesitation, insecurity and anxiety, bespeak the image of a man enslaved. Freedom lifts man to his Creator.

Exhilarating and inspiring, freedom is lost when not used. The responsibility of freedom is the responsibility to fidelity, first and foremost; to faithfulness toward our vocation as human beings. We must always be sure that we accept no role in life that would in any way make us less human and thereby less free.

The really free man knows no guilt, because he knows no violation of the spirit. Freedom was not given to us that we might be harassed by guilt, but rather that we might be creative and responsible. "By their works you shall know them," says the Master. So too, as Christ saw his freedom fulfilled in giving of himself, he taught us that our freedom might often entail sacrifice of ourselves for humanity. But he did not hesitate or cower before responsibility, so as his followers we need not fear.

These thoughts on freedom are so much more important to me than the sterile discussion of whether or not man possesses a free will and how the free will acts on our judgments. Christian freedom means liberation from rigid categories, external legalisms, and intellectual atrophy. We are free so that we can direct our spirits to rise to the call of the Creator.

8. DO YOU APPROVE OF HOW THE WORD "LOVE" IS CURRENTLY USED IN RELIGIOUS WRITINGS?

§   NO

The word "love" admits of so many definitions that it has become corrupted. The word has many biblical applications, the most important of which is that God is love.

Love used to mean the tendency of the soul toward goodness. Christian love implied a reflection of a Christ-centered soul toward God and his law.

The highest form of love is charity. I prefer the word "charity" to "love," for all charity is love but not all love is charity. Charity elevates love to the plane originally destined for it by God. Through charity, we are moved to love God above all things for His sake. Charity is patient, kind, and meek. St. Paul eloquently enshrined charity when he spoke about it in his epistles. People today who spout off about love do not have the same understanding as St. Paul.

Charity is not necessarily affection. I can be charitable toward someone without having to like him. I think this distinction is important, especially today when we are called to love everybody, to let anybody into our homes, offices, and factories. But we are really confusing love and giving it a dimension that is not found in the understanding of true charity. I can be charitable toward a person of another race or social group without having to shower him with affection. As a Christian, I try to show the common marks of Christian charity toward all, but I resent being forced to show personal affection toward any and everyone simply because I am a Christian.

Pope Paul says that if anyone wants to convert the world, he has first to love it. But some of the liberal priests give you the idea that you must put your arms around everyone. I try to follow the teachings of Pope Paul. I love my neighbor, but that love is something spiritual. It means that I desire good things for him, I wish him well. Although I try to respect all people, I cannot see love deteriorating into an emotional involvement with every person I meet.

I would like to see a return of the word "charity" in place of "love." I love my wife and my family; I show charity and respect for all others. By the same token, I expect those I meet, and those who make demands on me, to respect me, and if they choose, to give me some reason for going into a deeper and more charitable relationship with them. I have charity for my fellow man for the sake of God, because God is perfect and because God has been good to me.

❋ YES

Our love of all men is proof of our love for God. I only wish that the Church would pay more than lip service to true love. Perhaps the reason a lot of people are bothered by the discussions of love today is that we Catholics have too long been used to hiding our emotions and controlling our appetites. We have masked Christian life under the abstract term "charity." Now that the secular world has discovered the beauty and freshness of love, it is beating us at our own game. So, we find Christians either going overboard with affection or simply disdaining the vitality and openness of true love.

I reject the word "charity" because the word as formerly used within the Christian community implied an impersonal giving, a form of philanthropy, a detached offering of something rather than an involved concern with someone. To be charitable was to be patronizing. In other words, charity implied fulfilling an obligation rather than fulfilling one's humanity. Charity was practiced without real love.

Charity was a terrible concept that allowed one to pass judgment on another and publicly expose his faults, all under the guise of helping him grow spiritually. The alms-giving variety of charity was an affront to the dignity of the human being.

When we consider that God is love, that God acted "because he so loved the world," then we see the dynamic of love as an openness, a "kenosis," a true conversion toward another. It implies the gift of oneself in the act of giving. In other words, love cannot be detached, nor can it be objective or stand-offish. Dr. Karl Rahner explains love as a fulfillment in unselfishness and generosity whereby man imitates God's gift of himself to mankind through his Son.

We have difficulty with the concept of love. We are unable or unwilling to let our charity bear the mark of our personality. Since we are afraid to love all men personally, we stand off and hide behind a cold, abstract concept of charity. It is true that many young people see love as purely sentimental expression. But those who have difficulty accepting love in place of charity are victims of tradition. Sentiment and emotion are not evil, but human.

Christians have an obligation to love all men, especially our less-advantaged neighbors. Our love has to bear the seal of our personality; it has to be the best expression of that personality. Moreover we must put love into action, expressing it in genuine concern and interest.

Our love is exemplified in the Christian understanding of our Saviour and his life here on earth. He told us, "Greater love than this, no man hath, that he lay down his life for a friend." This kenosis, this emptying of ourselves on behalf of our brothers, is the key to real love. Without it, love becomes the detached charity of a disinterested Christianity.

The beauty of love is that it admits of a variety of expressions. But there must be a constancy in love, achieved through a fidelity to the example of Christ, the suffering Messiah.

9. DO YOU KNOW WHY THERE IS EVIL AND MISERY IN THE WORLD?

§ *YES*

Evil is the lack of goodness. God, who is all good, cannot be the cause of evil. Evil is human thought, speech, and action that is contrary to right reason and contrary to the laws of God and the Church. Earthquakes, floods, fire, and tornadoes are also evils, but God does not allow physical evils for their own sake. He permits them to happen for the same reason he allowed Job to suffer: to test our love and faith in him. God derives no joy from allowing suffering to touch us intimately. He allows these evils so that he can draw good from them.

St. Augustine tells us that God is powerful enough and good enough to make good even from evil. God seeks our spiritual good, and he allows us to lose our material goods at times so that our concerns can be redirected toward the spiritual. St. Paul tells us that earth is not our lasting home, but often a man becomes so attached to worldly goods that he forgets about God.

Once we understand the reality of God's providence and how he lovingly watches over our spiritual destiny, then we are not overly disturbed by the problem of evil. We can be sure that God's concern "reaches from end to end mightily and orders all things sweetly" [Wisdom 8:1].

Catholics believe that the world was made for the glory of God. He is not only the Creator, but the Conserver, the protector of all things. He sustains the world and protects it from dissolution. "In him we move and live and are" [Acts 17:27]. His concern for all creatures is unwavering. Not even a sparrow falls to the ground without his knowledge [Matthew 10:29]. Certainly, there are wars, but we have to remember who is in charge of the ship. We must have faith in God. Our concern should be to fulfill the laws of God and of the Church, and then everything else falls into place.

We were born to suffer, to undergo pain; through these purification processes we can move steadily toward our eternal goal. Better that we be about the business of the Lord, giving him homage and making proper use of his gifts here on earth, than worry about the existence of evil. It can have no power over us so long as we are in the state of grace and so long as we persevere under God's protection until the end. A deep faith in God and his divine providence enables us to have a healthy and realistic approach to the trials and tribulations of life.

✳ *NO*

I recognize that evil and misery exist, but I cannot accept or understand them. Evil and misery are opposed to a true God-concept, and they contradict the very nature of man. Man was made for progress and happiness. Although I do not blame God for man's ills, I do blame the upside-down God-concept of many Christians.

The existence of evil is something we cannot deny, but we can help alleviate it. The Creator placed us in the world, and he demands not a flight from reality, but rather a confrontation with it.

Whether evil is the absence of goodness or an active force, it is not removed by waving a magic wand. Evil in itself can have no independent reality. God endowed man with powers and insights to do good, but we have been too busy concentrating on our own needs and in our selfishness have lost sight of the divine call to increase and multiply our innate goodness. Man, not God, is at fault for the increasing evil in our world. When man ignores his personal freedom, when he hides behind the walls of religion to avoid the next world, when he allows other people to do his thinking for him, then he becomes blind to the power of God within himself, and this closes off another font of goodness for the human race. That's the nature of evil. Selfishness is generally the root of evil, a selfishness that causes a man to reject his own destiny, to exist passively, and to let others work toward removing the world's problems.

Floods, earthquakes, and disease are more difficult to understand. But even here we have a responsibility to work for the prevention of such evils. In 1955 a hurricane caused terrible floods along most of the East Coast. Careful analysis has since placed the cause of the floods at mankind's door, for man had failed to use his engineering ability to avoid catastrophe. Since that time, careful planning and the utilization of scientific techniques have diminished the possibility of a recurrence.

Today, thousands suffer and die from heart disease and

cancer, but one day man will be rid of such evil. Hundreds of thousands of dollars are being spent on research for a cancer cure and other medical breakthroughs. Man is diminishing the power of disease over his life. The hunger and backwardness of the migratory worker and ghetto dweller can also be corrected by the creative forces of a concerned mankind.

Evil, then, is a failure on the part of man to use his God-given powers. Anything—anything whatever—that sustains man in his inactivity is also evil. A boundless optimism in himself is the key to man's progress on earth. In fact, we can pay no greater tribute to God than to hail the arsenal of creativity with which he endowed his creatures. This homage, though, must include resourcefulness and achievement. Our God-concept must allow for growth and progress in the direction that Christ himself exemplified. When man lives away from himself, he abandons God. This, I believe, is the greatest evil. When man rejects his brother in order to concentrate on ritual and rite, he abandons God and perpetuates misery and moral evil. The Church has taught man to accept suffering and hardship. This is good, for we can find meaning even in suffering, but suffering is acceptable only after man has seriously applied his talents and intelligence to conquering it.

10. DO YOU THINK
    THE SOCIAL NATURE OF MAN
    IS OVEREMPHASIZED TODAY?

§ YES

St. Thomas teaches us that man has a social nature and an individual nature and that together these make up the person. Man is basically an individual. He acts as an individual and as such is responsible for his actions. Man, however, cannot live alone. And since he does need other people, he has a tendency to seek out people with similar tastes and goals. Today, however, we are being forced to accept a herd instinct, a common conscience and a majority ethic. This erroneous concept arises from a lack of understanding of man's social needs.

Because some men see life a certain way does not mean that all men are held to that same point of view. We see the consequences of this mistake in applications of the Church's social teaching. Some individuals would have us turn our government into a socialist state, and they are constantly advocating a welfare state where the group and not the individual gets top priority. The Church has taught us to respect the individual's point of view and especially to relate to God as an individual. The notion of morality is based on the supremacy of the individual. If following the crowd means violating the law of God in a particular action, the individual cannot plead innocence but must accept the consequences of his action.

Americans have been trained to respect the rights of the individual. Today, some priests would have us reject our former regard for the individual and accept an exaggeration of the social nature of man. I refuse to do this, since it is so much at odds with the true teachings of the Church on the nature of man. Atheistic communism has its origins in this exaggeration, and socialism leads to it. When the individual is lost in the herd, then we are in trouble. The mosaic of mankind is the variety of individuals, all of whom add their own particularity to the total picture. Remove any one of them and you leave a gaping hole.

I think you can exaggerate the role of the individual. After all, we do have need for one another. But in the final analysis, responsibility and initiative are rooted in the individual. I do not feel responsible for the mistakes of people I do not know. I do not feel the suffering and pain of people who live thousands of miles across the world. Nor am I ashamed to say this. I know of Martin Buber's teaching that we are supposed to relate to one another on an I-Thou plane. I try to do this, but I do this as an I. That I should accept a group mentality or a group conscience seems to me a distortion of the nature of man.

I deal with people as individuals, and I accept the consequences of my actions as an individual. I try to practice charity toward all, but I view my efforts as controlled and dictated by the basic needs I experience as an individual. This is not egotism, for egotism is an unwillingness to help. I act to protect myself, knowing that if I am absorbed into a communal concept, then, more than likely, the unrealism inherent in such a concept would eventually leave me as an individual unprotected and at the mercy of fate. Responsibility, merit, conscience, and God make no sense otherwise.

✳ NO

We Catholics have, until recent times, been individualistic, and thus have become immobile because we canonized a one-to-one relationship with God at the expense of the needs of humanity. As persons, we are both one and many, and this is our power for good.

In his memorable encyclical *Peace on Earth* Pope John XXIII said that we are all members of the human family, and that this is the will of God. A society in which the family is considered the fundamental unit spotlights man's social dimension. The fear of losing one's identity and power as an individual through social emphasis is real. But membership in the human family is achieved through preserving man's individuality. Man cannot escape his social obligations, but neither can he reject his link with the human family. Pope John saw the enigma of Christianity in the millions that go to bed hungry each night and other millions that look the other way. This sight of Christians turning away from social consciousness pained him.

Pope Paul, in his encyclical *The Development of Peoples,* also emphasized man's obligation to help one another. Americans especially need this reminder that "we are all brothers," and that we must sensitize our consciences in the light of genuine Christianity. If one examines the nature of the Church itself, one sees the communal structure it reveals; the term *ecclesia* itself bespeaks community. The command of Christ to go forth and witness to all nations underlies the social aspect of Christianity. Christ identified with the entire human family and gave his life for its betterment. The reality of love is not often understood as dependent upon action consonant with love's goals. Concern for others is vital to the very concept of love. When Christ was asked about the greatest commandment, he told us that we must love our neighbor as ourselves; in this statement he joined the individual and social obligations of man's nature. We must strike a happy balance and yet not view our Christian obligation as purely self-aggrandizement.

When Christ depicted the Last Judgment, he illustrated the Christian obligation to perform works of mercy. When we feed the hungry, clothe the naked, visit the imprisoned, and give alms to the needy, we help others fulfill their human nature. Pope Paul expressed the true concept of Christian love in paragraph 23 of *The Development of Peoples*: "If someone who has the riches of this world sees his brother in need and closes his heart to him, how does the love of God abide in him. . . . To quote St. Ambrose: 'You are not making a gift of your possessions to the poor person. You are handing over to him what is his. For what has been given in common for the use of all, you have arrogated to yourself. The world is given to all, and not only to the rich.' No one is justified in keeping for his exclusive use what he does not need when others lack necessities." Love demands all, and in the fulfillment of love we discover our true selves.

The new theology has enriched us all in emphasizing our social obligations, and at the same time has led us to a more realistic appreciation of what we are and why we move in God.

III

GOD

FROM EARLIEST DAYS man has been under the shadow of God. Even today, in our scientific era, we are constantly looking over our shoulder to see if God is present. This preoccupation of man finds expression in his culture, for from the beginning he has tried to picture God. God has most often been given the form and characteristics of man—a superman, indeed, but a man. In the early culture of the East, God was a warrior, a vibrant, fiery young man. He seemed almost impetuous in his anger and his passions. This is true even of the Hebrew God. Later, in the early and middle Christian era, God became the Father, the man with the great wisdom and the white beard. He was the wise old sage who loved us all, but still demanded much from us. Our present culture has simply extended these analogies: first God was a young man, then he became the old Father, and now he's dead! He is simply a corpse, some claim, that insecure people seek to carry around with them, like a Linus blanket. God had life and purpose at one time but now he's dead.

This, of course, is a simplification of the situation. After all, God is a spirit, and thus is not affected by the vicissitudes of physcal life. The Church teaches us that. Instead of "picturing" God, the Church tried to intellectualize him. Our salvation depends solely on our union with God. To be united with him, we must know who he is. As the official spokesman for God, the Church has taken on the job of teaching us, through a detailed theology of the nature of God. God is spirit, God is one, yet made up of three distinct persons; he is eternal, unchanging; he is all-powerful, all-knowing; he is goodness, truth, beauty. Our union with God is brought about by imitation of his perfections: "Be perfect as thy heavenly Father is perfect." It is hard to understand these divine attributes, but that is the challenge of our God-man relationship. (Of course, little can be done by us alone; God has to help us relate to him.) We must accept the God that has been given us by our Church. As time goes on, however, we will be able to get a better understanding of who and what God is, because God—

perfection himself—unchangingly waits to be discovered for what he is.

Both culture and Church have attributed a special personality to God. And we simply have to change our attitudes and our very beings to conform to the God they have painted for us. With this kind of system we do not have much opportunity to relate to God as a person. Whether we like it or not, the dynamics of personal relationships are all-important in our society today. But the traditional views of God do not offer us an opportunity to realize the uniqueness of our own personality. What the Church seems to be saying is this: "Don't get too close. We'll take care of it for you. You just listen to us. Don't call us, we'll call you."

Do you think you've been waiting long enough for that call to come? Are you going to wait any longer for the Church to decide who God will be?

1. IS GOD DEAD?

§ NO

He is not dead. That is a contradiction in terms. God, by his very nature, is eternal and always relevant. Many knowledgeable people today are saying that God is dead. I'm not saying they are in bad faith (although some of them might very well be), but they are misguided. They have forgotten that the teachings of the Church about God is God's very word, and thus is eternally true.

The whole universe, our very lives, our very breath depend on God's constant interest and concern. Even if it were possible that he could die, then we too would cease to exist. Since we're here, God must be also.

People say that when they talk about the death of God they mean the demise of his moral and ethical influence over the lives of men. That is absurd. Without God, man would have no direction, no purpose. Without God to correct him, man would degenerate into a beast, no better. Man's only claim to morality is his union with God. Morality is God.

Perhaps we must reflect on our idea of God, but we must never lose sight of who God is: the Supreme Being who has total control over the whole universe. His will is the last word, and nothing—nothing at all—happens without his knowing about it. God can never die.

✳ YES

God is dead; that is, the traditional God is dead. This traditional God is a combination of myths and fables. He is made up of the hopes of men, men frightened by the unsureness of life, and the certainty of death. He is the God who is the opiate of the people, who allows people to look toward some future—and quite nebulous—life after death while thumbing their noses at the problems of this life. This God is dead.

The God that will arise from the corpse of the traditional God will be real. He will be dynamic; he will be free, free in every sense: free from all necessity and free from any characterizations that the Church might try to force upon him and us. When this God arises, then it will finally be true to say that God is our God and we are his people.

2. COULD GOD EXIST WITHOUT MAN?

§ YES

Because God is eternal, he of course existed before man. He is totally independent of any temporal thing. He made the world freely. He did not have to do it. He does not have to keep it in existence. Our existence is totally contingent, totally dependent on the will of God. God does not depend on man at all.

Even in the world of men, man is not absolutely necessary. God can accomplish his will without man's help. Usually God is patient enough to let man do most of the work. But this can be looked upon as a favor to man from God. It increases man's dignity to be allowed to participate in God's work. But man, by doing too much, can get in the way of the work of God. Every man must promote justice. But men should remember that it is they who need God's help, not God who needs theirs.

✳ NO

It is true that God certainly did exist before us, because he created us. But he has chosen to make us necessary. He put us on earth and told us to make it grow, and so the responsibility is ours. If we don't do it, nobody will, and God's plan will be foiled. Such an idea does no injustice to God's greatness; it rather enhances his power. He has chosen to let tremendous responsibility rest on our shoulders.

If we were to deal totally in the abstract, in theory, we might conclude that God could do without us. But we are here on earth in vast numbers, and we are here to stay (unless, of course, we blow ourselves off the face of the earth with our bombs; but even then it is our decision). In that sense, God has no choice but to let us continue what he himself started: human destiny.

When John Kennedy said that God's work must truly be our own, I think he meant that unless we do that work, it won't be done. This belief increases in us the realization of our responsibility to help God. This belief helps us establish a better union with God.

3. DOES GOD CHANGE?

§ NO

God's unchangeableness is one of the most important points of my relationship to him and to the Church. It is one of the basic premises of our culture and our civilization. If God were to change, what would happen? Would truth change, would goodness change, would beauty change? If they changed, who would decide what they were changed to? How would we know anything? We would be like an anchorless ship at sea, tossed and turned by any wave of criticism and doubt. God's unchangeableness is the anchor. If our belief in that steadfastness is taken away, there will be no way to be sure, no way to know the truth.

Why is there so much confusion in the world today? Because

people refuse to believe in God. They don't know what to believe and thus accept any will-of-the-wisp orator who comes along. Unless we build on the rock of faith, we will be building on sand.

✳ YES

People who say that God cannot and does not change understand the word "change" in the Greek philosophical sense. Greek thinkers believed that if a thing could change or move, it was not complete, since it had a tendency or potency toward something else. Therefore God, who is complete in every sense, cannot change. He is eternally complete. Today in our civilization, "change" has a more positive and general sense. Change is a natural and healthy part of any dynamic relationship. God of his own accord has set up a relationship with man, and thus as the relationship develops he changes. This could be just an argument in semantics, since no one can enter the mind of God, but for a dynamic person such a notion of change is of the utmost importance. Because of this, we don't have to give up our personality in order to approach an unchanging, set God. We can be ourselves and meet God as a person. Change affects God just as it affects everything.

4. DO WE HAVE TO BELIEVE IN GOD?

§ YES

I think that the existence of God is evident to anyone who is sincere. The Church has taught us many examples of the proof of God's existence: the order in the universe, the beauty of nature, and the fact that the universe had to start somewhere.

This, of course, is only a natural belief in God. But everyone on this earth has a natural belief in God, just like their belief that the sun will rise tomorrow or the clock will strike six times at six o'clock. There is no special merit in this kind of natural belief, as everyone who is honest has it.

But God alone can give us supernatural belief. He gives it only to selected people and, often enough, people refuse this great and awesome gift. When they refuse it, they are without excuse. When they accept it, they must accept it in its entirety. None of this "I love your Christ, but I hate your Christians." If this gift is given to a person, he has to accept it. Otherwise he is morally wrong.

✳ NO

Men do not necessarily have to believe in God. We must remember that we are all part of the human condition. A man's outlook on life and on the most important part of life—his relationship to a supreme being—is colored by his environment. Our society today does not lend itself readily to belief in God, especially the belief held by organized religion. Not everyone is capable of realizing on his own that religion can often get in the way of God. He is told to accept it all or none of it, and often he accepts none of it.

Faith, belief in God, is a unique aspect in our lives. Faith has been called a leap in the dark. When you leap in the dark, you're really not sure if there's going to be anything solid where you land. We take this kind of leap when we drive through an intersection and assume that the other fellow is going to stop for the red light. In another sense we take a leap when we plan our next day, not really knowing if we will wake up in the morning. We have to take these little leaps. Otherwise we would never begin anything for fear that we might not finish, and why waste our time?

Belief in God has been called the "great leap." It reflects a basic attitude we take toward life, and it is simply one choice among several. If you don't believe in God, you'll look on life in one way. If you do believe in God, your whole outlook will be different. Either way, your whole life is affected. Not everyone is able to take this leap on his own. And I feel that if he can't do it freely he shouldn't do it. But I also believe that, given the proper opportunities and environment, every person would be willing to take this "great leap" of faith because God truly has made himself

known to this world. This is a challenge to those of us who already
have accepted God in our lives.

5. DOES GOD HAVE A PLAN FOR THE UNIVERSE?

§ YES

This is what we talk about when we mention the *will* of God.
I've been taught all my life to follow God's will, to make myself
available to God's will. And I've been told that we can find out
what God's will is by listening to the Church. The Church holds
the key to salvation.

This makes sense, of course. God has to give us some sort of
direction, and once he gives it, he can't very well change his mind.
So I guess you can call it a plan. It's the job of every Catholic, and
every other person, to find out where he fits into God's plan and
then fit himself into it. That's why, I guess, they say of a person
who has left the seminary or the convent: "It just wasn't in God's
plan." By fitting ourselves into the eternal plan of God, then, we
are best fulfilling our Christian responsibility.

This does not mean, though, that we are predestined. We
can always foil God's plan in our lives. But the overall plan
(which, of course, is much more important than just you or me)
can never fail, because God cannot be outdone.

✳ NO

When I hear people talking about a plan, I picture a detailed
program with all the steps from beginning to end written out and
notarized. I think that God, by leaving us on this earth by ourselves, has shown his willingness to let us guide our own destinies.
This is not anarchy; this is creative responsibility. We certainly
have a goal. This was given to us by Christ. But note that God
became man before he freely proposed this goal. And even then
he didn't lay down any detailed program for achieving it. If this

fact is fully accepted, then we will accomplish more than if we attempted to fit ourselves into a program. Simply to follow a set pattern is less courageous and less effective than to strike out boldly in new endeavors in an attempt to accomplish the goal set before us: to love one another as Christ loved us.

6. DO YOU KNOW WHO JESUS CHRIST IS?

§ YES

Whenever I think of Jesus Christ, I think of the real presence in the Eucharist. The Church teaches us that Christ is present, whole and entire, under the appearance of bread and wine. This is the Christ I have related to all my life—the Christ I know through faith. In my prayers and in my thoughts, I always picture Christ in the tabernacle. Christ said to doubting St. Thomas that those who saw were blessed, but more blessed were they who have not seen and yet have believed. I attend Mass often and try to be a daily communicant so that Christ will dwell within me throughout the day. The Benediction of the Blessed Sacrament, where the Host is placed in a monstrance and offered for our adoration and praise, the hymns, and the spirit of the entire sacred ceremony all help me to feel Christ's presence.

I meditate often on the image of the suffering Saviour. The Way of the Cross is particularly meaningful to me. For me, this is the real life of Christ, written in his pain and blood. The Gospel that tells this story comes to life for me in the Way of the Cross. I would love to go to Jerusalem, to see the very land where Jesus lived and died, to walk the bloody way of Calvary. Jesus is the second person of the Blessed Trinity, but he is also my Saviour and my teacher.

I have a meaningful rapport with Jesus, and I feel I know who he is. Reading the Scriptures helps me hear him speak to me. I am saddened by the attempts of some people to explain away the Eucharist, which is the center of our religion, the font of our strength, and the power of our faith. I have never seen Christ, yet

I know he is present in our tabernacles, and through this faith I am able to relate personally to him. Nothing is difficult for me, nothing is too much of a sacrifice. I look forward to the day when I can meet my God face to face in the beatific vision, yet I am content to experience his goodness and his presence in my life today.

❋ *NO*

I do not know who Jesus Christ is. I remember what the Church teaches about him, that he is God and the second person of the Blessed Trinity, and that he is present in the Eucharist. But this is not the Christ that I know. The Christ I know is found in me and in my brother. Vatican II offers us a new image of Christ and a broader variety of presence. Whereas we were led to believe simply in the eucharistic presence, the Council showed us that Christ is also found in the Scriptures and in the person of our brother.

Some people feel that in searching out new dimensions of the presence of Christ, we are thereby rejecting the traditional presence. On the contrary, I find my faith in the Eucharist deepened by a keener awareness of Christ in my brother. The celebration of the mystery of Christ's death and resurrection takes on a greater significance when performed in an atmosphere of love and respect for one another. I don't think that we have adequately approached the reality of Christ's presence. We are beginning to think of him more and more in terms of his humanity, without forgetting his divine origin. Jesus the man, the carpenter, the traveler, the physician, is so much easier to relate to than Jesus, Lord and Saviour. What is important is what Christ did for mankind, and the manner in which he accomplished his mission. These human aspects of Christ are portrayed so much more realistically for us today than in the past.

Christ the High Priest, the Wonder Worker, the flashing meteor never appealed to me. I was amazed and I was awed, but I was not inspired to follow him, because he came across as one who was out of my class. Imitating Christ was usually a physical impossibility for one less than a superman. I think the current stress on the Incarnation, the fact that God took man's flesh and nature, this central reality of Christianity wherein the ordinary was made important and vital, well, it all made a difference. You want to pitch in and finish where he left off. This is what Christianity really is all about. The Church is supposed to be the extension of Christ, the work of Christ. As members of the Church, we share in his mission, which is to fulfill mankind. Christ came not only to save mankind, but to direct mankind toward greater fulfillment.

What was Christ saving mankind from? From man? But he was part of mankind, and furthermore, mankind was his father's creation. Man's imperfection, his weakness if you will, arises from his unwillingness or inability to fulfill himself, to become everything that God intended. The more human we become, the more Christlike we become, for through the Incarnation Christ became a perfect man. I really don't know who Christ is, but that does not bother me. I think religion should be the act of searching for Christ and experiencing one another's humanity in that search.

Do we ever really know a fellow human being? We think we know our close friends, our families, and yet they consistently surprise us, and that is the beautiful thing about life. Friendships do not grow stale, but deepen with each revealing dimension. So too with Christ. I think about the ghettos and the hunger patches of our earth. I know Christ is there somewhere. And he is suffering and he is lonely just as he was once many years ago. He is in pain, not because fewer visits to the Blessed Sacrament are being made, but because fewer men take the trouble to discover the reality of Christ in their neighbor. Christ's Gospel is worth meditating about, but what is more important is how we respond to that Gospel—what we do with it, and where we go. It's a lifetime's work, finding, relating to, and getting to know the real Christ, but despite the difficulty I find it worthwhile. Perhaps I'll never get to know Christ in this world, but I'll spend my time searching. He gave us lots of hints in the Gospels. He was poor, he was lonely, he was compassionate: and he was thoroughly human.

7. IS THE INCARNATION IMPORTANT TO YOU?

§ YES

If God had not conceived of the Incarnation as necessary he would not have acted upon it. That God would consider lowering himself to become man, to imprison himself in human flesh, to take on the human limitations of life on earth, shouts the importance of the Incarnation. This is the prime example of the mercy, the all-loving mercy, of the Creator for his creatures. This is the hope of our religion, that despite the constant turning away from God, despite the idolatrous blasphemy that was heaped on him, God would choose to save the human race, which did not begin to deserve such merciful redemption.

When one thinks of the humble beginnings of Jesus and the abuse and insults he had to endure to prove God's love of man, one cannot but see the huge unpayable debt that each of us owes to our Creator because of the Incarnation. God so loved the world that he gave his only begotten Son to redeem it. More than that, he further expressed his love by allowing his Son to be born into wretched and humble conditions and to suffer inhuman torture and death. "Greater love than this no man hath than to lay down his life for a friend." But exceedingly greater love no God could have than to permit his Son to lead the most abhorrent existence.

"The word was made flesh, and dwelt among us." The word came to man so that man might become worthy of the promises of Christ. If there is to be any hope for humanity today, it must rest in the realization of God's great love and mercy.

Throughout the history of mankind, no greater example of God's great love can be found than in the Incarnation and death of our Lord and Saviour Jesus. Redeeming mankind and giving it its one chance for salvation was an overwhelming task, and it demanded the greatest price. God did not shrink from that task; he became man, lived as man, and paid the price of the supreme sacrifice. The debt for our salvation was so immeasurable that only the most priceless ransom could meet the cost. This in itself cannot but overawe us with the importance of the Incarnation, the greatest ransom of all time, upon which our faith is founded. For many Catholics, Christ's terrible agony and crucifixion is indeed the cornerstone of their faith.

Yet it must be seen that even overshadowing the crucifixion was the complete abandon and humble servitude of the divinity, allowing himself to be transformed into human existence yet keeping his divinity intact. It is when we look at this awesome mystery of the Incarnation that we begin to understand what an important role it must play in the understanding of our Christian heritage and our eternal salvation.

✳ NO

Not in the traditional sense. In the past when the Church spoke of the Incarnation it referred to God being transformed into living humanity in the person of Jesus Christ. On this the Church rested its claim as the one true Church, the way of salvation. However, to a real Catholic the basic importance of life is to live what Christ stood for. To make the all-important reason for existence rest solely on Christ's divinity is to short-change Christ himself, that is, the life he led and the teachings he espoused.

For a real Catholic love of God and love of neighbor are the firm grounds of salvation. To do what Christ said solely because he was God is a negativistic approach. It is to go with a winner, so to speak. If this traditional understanding of Christianity continues, the Church is headed toward destruction because its concept of Christ's Incarnation is a very selfish one. Perhaps this is one of the reasons that the Church of the past remained within narrow, self-righteous boundaries, and that the practicing Catholic we often encounter is the kind of person who goes to Mass, says his prayers, "belongs" to the Church, yet makes no protest when the basic principles of Christianity are trampled on.

Perhaps a good test might be this: If tomorrow it was conclusively shown that Christ was not God, that the Incarnation was not a reality in the most literal sense, how many Catholics might be shaken? How many would be able to go on loving their neighbor, leading honest lives, and believing in the dignity of man and the necessity of loving one another as Christ loved us? He loved us whether he was God or not. In other words, if this selfish idea of being with the winner is interpreted as the basic foundation of our faith, it can only foster more selfishness in those who believe on these grounds.

The real worth of the Incarnation to Catholics today, if it is to have a value, must be to see in it the great worth that the Creator placed upon the created, the great dignity and basic value of being human. It is to appreciate that God freely chose to become part of the human race to help this image and likeness of himself, this integral part of himself, to fulfill its destiny. God united himself with mankind from the first person he created to the last person he will create. The Incarnation must be seen as the catalyst that God used to demonstrate the divine-human continuity, with all the responsibilities and challenges thereby implied by this most complete act of love that God could show to his creation.

8.   WAS CHRIST A PROPHET?

§   NO

Christ was not a prophet in the traditional sense of the term. Jeremiah, Jonas, Isaiah, and the others were prophets, but Christ was the person about whom the prophets spoke. Fundamentally, a prophet is a witness to God's revelation. Christ is God and therefore greater than the prophets.

Today many people are quick to term any charismatic or mysterious person a prophet. They refer to Christ as a prophet, which is dangerous because it obscures his divinity. There is also a danger of minimizing Christ's role in the redemption through too loose a usage of the term "prophet." Some have put Christ on the same footing as Gandhi, Mohammed, and even John F. Kennedy, referring to them as dynamic prophets. Where will it all end, if we demythologize even the Son of God?

"Prophecy" implies the telling of the future. Christ did not spend his time reading the future for the Jews, nor did he use enigmatic language and heavy symbolism as did the prophets of the Old Testament. His language was direct and to the point, as witness his Sermon on the Mount.

The prophets of both the Old and New Testament and even those of our own time are valuable to mankind, but only as they help us relate to God. Christ was first and foremost God, the Saviour. His life, death, and resurrection were a fulfillment of the prophecies. Prophecy can at times be erroneous because the prophet, being human, is subject to error. This possibility cannot exist for Christ, because Christ was God and God is infallible. Let us respect the prophets, but let us beware lest in exalting them we fall into the error of humanizing Christ to the detriment of his divinity.

Divine Revelation came to an end with John the Apostle. We can learn nothing new from the budding crop of prophets who seek a special kinship with Christ. We should rather seek our inspiration and spiritual nourishment in the words of Christ, and in the biblical figures whose prophecies he fulfilled.

❋ YES

A prophet is one who reveals God and his message to man. Jesus, who was both God and man, supremely illustrates the role of prophet. In his person he expressed God, and in his life he exemplified the divine reality for man. It is true that overemphasis on the prophetic nature of Christ could lead to confusion, but understanding Christ as prophet presents the Christian with a tangible and inspirational dimension of his Saviour.

The lives of great men who have helped mankind often evoke a vision of Christ. Vatican II was not inclined to reject the charismatic influence of our leaders. The magnetism of the prophet concept is incredible. People ask "Who is Christ?" and immediately, upon recalling his salutary influence through the ages, they are struck with one thought: *He is a prophet.*

Even the simple story of the woman at the well vividly portrays the effect Christ had on people. A prophet is pictured as a holy man, one who helps people, and who directs them toward the safe and sure ways of life. Our age is a sad age because not enough attention is accorded those who speak on behalf of man.

This is the role of the prophet. Who speaks on behalf of man today? Who speaks against injustice, greed, useless slaughter, and the rabid rush for power? Very few indeed. And yet if we open our minds and hearts, we can see Christ the prophet walking among us, trying to make himself heard among the pushing, rushing hordes. Those who speak on behalf of the Negro are prophets, since they are trying to save us from ourselves. Those who offer their lives for peace, even to the extent of risking imprisonment, they too are prophets.

Someone has said that no one has time to listen any more. Everyone seems in a hurry, rushing off somewhere because he has to be someplace to meet someone. But the voice of the prophet makes us stop and look at ourselves. It causes us to wonder. This is what Christ did in his time. He disturbed the status quo and gave his life so that his voice might ring through the ages. People expect prophets to foretell the future, and, in a way, prophets do just that. But they foretell the future by decrying the evils of the present, warning us of disastrous paths.

If we have great prophets today, and we do, if we have prophetic insights bursting into our reveries and wishful thinking, it's because the message of Jesus the prophet is still heard. As the great prophet, Christ is the measure of today's prophets. He stands as an example to all of us who tend to forget why he came to earth. He is an inspiration and a guide to those of us who would make his life and death not in vain.

9. DO YOU STILL PRACTICE DEVOTION TO THE SACRED HEART?

§ YES

Many Catholics used to go to Mass and communion on the first Friday of every month, in veneration of the Sacred Heart of Jesus. The priests heard confessions on Thursday evenings until late into the night, and the children of the parish schools would attend Mass and sing special hymns on the first Fridays. The first Friday used to be something special.

In the evening there was Benediction of the Blessed Sacrament, and the priest would read a beautiful consecration of the whole human race to the Sacred Heart; but those days seem to be gone. The churches are nearly empty on first Friday now, and few pay any attention to the Sacred Heart. Some new theologians accuse the Church of having been too sentimental toward the person of Christ, and they cite devotion to the Sacred Heart as a prime example.

The object of this devotion seems to me to be unquestionable, as it brings people into a very personal relationship with Christ. It emphasizes his humanity and the terrible tortures he underwent out of love of mankind.

The sentiments of some "new liturgies" turn me off more than devotion to the Sacred Heart ever could. At least such devotion did not stress the heart for the heart's sake alone, but was veneration of Christ's total sacred body, and ultimately the divine person housed in that body. The heart was revered because the heart is the symbol of love, just as the lily represents purity. In singling out the heart of Christ, we were really stressing the mercy and goodness of the Creator. The Church has always cherished devotion to the Sacred Heart and encouraged it. The devotion was offered so that Catholics might be motivated to carry out their duties of love and promote their spiritual enrichment.

✳ NO

Devotion to the Sacred Heart was a period piece, appropriate only for a particular era in history. It no longer fulfills its original purpose; it does not attract people to a deeper understanding of the person of Christ. Today the devotion appeals only to the unsophisticated.

Ours is a scientific age. Emphasis on the Sacred Heart does not make sense today, for we are more literal and more realistic, but the fact that one rejects the symbolism of this devotion cannot be construed as a denial of the reality of Christ. Concentration on anatomy is not spiritually elevating. Religion can no longer inspire childlike beliefs; today people have a more mature grasp of the principles motivating a dedication to a God-figure. We want to relate to God on a realistic level, to know the ideology of Christ and the why of his actions. Our acceptance of religion is both personal and scientific, for we are creatures of our times.

In analyzing the maturation process in the updating of religion, it is important to understand why a particular form of devotion is put aside, and also to ascertain how another, more contemporary element might be introduced. No one should condemn a person because he finds a formerly revered devotion meaningless any more than a progressive person should condemn one who finds solace in the traditional devotions. One should understand that a person sincerely bent on establishing a meaningful relationship with Christ must necessarily be selective in the devotions he adopts. It is hardly Christian to castigate another person because he relates to Christ in a way that is not appealing to us. So long as Christians respect one another's freedom of expression and allow selectivity in nonessentials, then a healthy climate for diversity and initiative will prevail. Religion makes enough demands upon a person's conscience, without making him conform in his private devotions and optional religious expressions.

St. Paul tells us that what is important is Jesus Christ, first, last, and always. The mature Christian must be left free to explore how and in what way he wants to relate to Christ. But his selectivity in optional areas must not be condemned. Christ tells us to judge justly, and to judge no man. There was a time when devotion to the beard of Joseph and the milk of Mary was going strong in the Church. Rejection of a mode of devotion is not necessarily a rejection of God, who must always remain the object of our attention and imitation.

10. DO YOU BELIEVE IN MIRACLES?

§ YES

Miracles reflect the power of God, who is all-powerful. A miracle is a proof that God does not have to offer. He performs miracles because man is hardened and feels he needs proof of a divine being. Christ never performed a miracle unless it was necessary. And if somone *demanded* that he show his divinity, as did the high priests and Pharisees, Christ generally ignored them. Christ's walking upon the water, curing the sick, and raising the dead were miracles. His own resurrection was a miracle. We accept the fact that Christ, being God, could perform miracles.

Many people scoff at miracles and attribute them to mysterious causes. It always strikes me as strange that these cynics attribute to some "mysterious, unknown cause" what they would deny to some known and definite cause, God. In our own time we have been blessed with many miracles, such as those at Lourdes, Fatima, and Guadalupe, Mexico. I've even read that there are many miracles attributed to Pope John XXIII—cases that have been offered as testimony of his saintliness before the throne of God. Pius X, the Pope of the Eucharist, was able to bilocate, or be in two places at one time. He was seen in other parts of the world when he was present in the Vatican. Pius XII is also said to have had miraculous powers.

Scientists contend that miracles are against the laws of nature because they contradict nature. But isn't it reasonable to assert that the Lord and Master of the universe, who established the laws of nature, has the power to suspend these laws or allow them to operate in another fashion? Such is the case with miracles.

The great medical scientist Alexis Carrel had his faith renewed at the grotto of Lourdes. He had denied the possibility of a cure for a woman who was at death's door. But the scientist humbly admitted the power of God when the woman was cured through the intercession of Our Lady of Lourdes.

Miracles are possible because they happen, and we have medical testimony to confirm the occurrence of miracles in our times. Miracles are performed by God to draw men to him, and they are a concession to man's need for signs. An evil and adulterous generation demands a sign, the Gospel says. And so God allows for wondrous shows of his omnipotence. The very existence of the Catholic faith down through history is also a miracle. For despite men's attempts to crush the one, holy, Catholic, and apostolic Church, the Church triumphs.

※ NO

The wooden birds that fly in the apocryphal writings, the five hundred white lions and the dragon-drawn chariot of Buddha, the moon-dividing of Mohammed, Christ walking upon the waters, all of these are merely symbols of some religious teaching. They make a point, and the point is more important than the symbol. I don't deny the possibility of these phenomena, which may not have an accessible explanation. You can call them miracles if you will. I believe that these phenomena have taken place, but I am loath to accept the explanation behind miracles—that they have a cause outside man and nature. St. Thomas and others have cautioned that we should not multiply entities unnecessarily. If something can have a natural explanation, why should we be so eager to evoke some mystical intervention?

The things we do today, such as drive cars, fly in jet-propelled aircraft, walk in space, transplant hearts, were unthinkable in the last century. Man matures in his own understanding of himself and his powers, and, through that maturation process, he is able to achieve what at some other time in history may have been considered impossible—just as we today find it difficult to project ourselves into the next thousand years and imagine the possible forms and ways of life.

Religion has thrived on the concept of the mysterious, complete with totems and tabus and castes. The wider man's horizon and industry, the less need he has for the mysterious, for witchcraft. Emphasis on man's native industry, far from detracting from the power of God, serves to enhance God's omnipotence. The natural is the product of God, and why hide behind the supernatural when faced with what strikes us as inexplicable? A few years ago the Catholic world was pained that a religious writer would chide Catholic University because it did not produce the scientists and intellectuals responsible for daring explorations into medicine, space, and atomic energy. Where are the Catholic Oppenheimers, he cried. Although the question might be considered naïve and arrogant, the writer did underscore the fact that Catholic intellectuals are not in the avante-garde legions braving the unknown. Catholics are instinctively safe in the realm of the supernatural. Miracles prove a convenient shield to stave off the inquiries of an otherwise restless intellect.

The atheistic doctor and scientist have given more glory to God through their contributions to mankind's health and happiness than have all the pious mutterings about miracles.

THE WORLD
WE LIVE IN

"THE MORE I GO into the world, the less of a man I become." Remember that saying? It is a paraphrase of a statement attributed to Thomas à Kempis, author of the *Imitation of Christ*. In a real sense, it represents the basic attitude of the Church toward the world.

How has this outlook on life affected you? Has it created a conflict in your life between things of the Church and those of the world? Even the very word "secular," which derives from the Latin word meaning "world," is opposed to the realities of the spirit.

Many sermons have been delivered warning Catholics to beware of the world, a place of sin and debauchery, where one's virtue could become tainted or destroyed! The world crucified our Saviour. The world stood for everything evil. How fortunate Catholics were to have the Church, which protected them from the lures and pitfalls of worldliness.

But God created the world and put us in it. In hating the world, we hate our home. Running away from it into the sanctuary of the Church is supposed to make the Catholic good and special. But we can't escape the world. Our friends, family, possessions— all are in the world.

Is the world really opposed to God and goodness? Cannot a humanistic worldliness achieve some good? What about our science, our technology, our philanthropy? Is the world really all evil?

1. IS THERE A REAL DEFINITION OF THE WORLD?

§ YES

The Gospels teach that the world is opposed to the spirit, that it is a stumbling block to the world we hope to inhabit, heaven. St. Paul tells us that we are pilgrims, strangers, sojourners, and that we have no lasting kingdom on earth. Christ died to save the world, but the world rejected him: "He came unto his own and his own received him not." The great Church writers define the world as lusting after the things of the flesh and as the home of the devil. Experience teaches us that if we abandon our religious practices, it isn't long before we become enamored of worldly things. Our values become false, our interests center on the material, and we soon forget God and all he did for us. Many people think they can allow themselves to be caught up in the pleasures of the world and that on their deathbed God will grant them the grace of final repentance.

The seven deadly sins epitomize the world and all it stands for. God set up a standard for us to follow in the life of his divine Son, Jesus. If we are not willing to live up to the doctrine of Christ, if we prefer the ways of the world, then we will lose our soul. What does it profit a man if he gain the whole world and suffer the loss of his immortal soul?

Even Christ was tempted by the world, but he gathered the strength to repel Satan. He knew that the things of the world are passing and their pleasure fleeting. He taught us to dedicate our lives to pursuing our eternal salvation.

❀ NO

There is no real definition of the "world." The term has been used as a whipping boy, a scapegoat, by many people. People hurt themselves by condemning the world, for to abhor the world is to abhor oneself, one's home, and one's situation. If God really created the world, why should the representatives of God turn against it? Freud claimed that the Church set up a father image in God, and then enticed people into the Church with pie-in-the-sky promises.

How many evils have been perpetrated, how many injustices tolerated under the fiction that injustices are to be expected since the world is evil? More and more people in the Church today are demanding that priests define what they mean by "the world." Scriptures that were previously used to castigate the world are now found to have been twisted and bent to serve the purpose of puritanical, pessimistic churchmen of the past. Flee the world and you end in escapism. Flee the world and you avoid your responsibility.

2. DID CHRIST REALLY DISDAIN HIS EARTHLY SURROUNDINGS?

§ YES

Christ came into the world to redeem it, to change it. He told us he came to start a revolution, to set brother against brother. He did not come to destroy the law but to fulfill it. His attitude toward the standards of the world and its riches is proverbial. He did not seek power, he did not seek to be king of the Jews, although the Jews forcibly tried to make him king. He allowed his voice to ring with anger at the money changers in the temple, and it seems to me he set forth the separation of world and Church quite clearly when he said, "Render to Caesar the things that are Caesar's and to God the things that are God's."

Christ had a merciful attitude toward sinners, because he distinguished between the sinner and the sin. His lesson of charity was an enigma to the Jewish people. Whereas they were taught to seek vengeance and to withhold forgiveness, Christ taught his followers that it was the will of his Father that they forgive seven times seventy.

Jesus sent his seventy-two disciples out into the world without scrip or staff, so that they would not develop any worldly attachments. His entire mien was that of a man who was in the world, but not of it. He was a man with a mission who gave of himself completely to prepare his Father's kingdom. Even on the cross, Christ calmly reminded his persecutors that his kingdom was not of this world.

Christ was the light of the world. He had no need for the material comforts and distractions so eagerly sought by the so-called apostles of the twentieth century.

✳ *NO*

It is inconceivable that Christ would give up his heavenly existence and enter into the world with the purpose of helping man and yet disdain that world. Christ was the Son of God. He freely accepted to enter on a mission for the benefit of mankind. Would he despise the very situation within which he was to work?

People have too long distorted Christ's vision of the world. They have made his words inconsonant with his actions and his mission.

Christ's love of the world is shown in his parables. He used material things to lift man's gaze to God—the lilies of the field, the fishes, the bread on the waters. Far from loathing his Father's handiwork, he taught men to find the imprint of God in themselves and in the world around them.

Why has the Church wanted Christ to exist in some sort of vacuum? Why do people set up a dialectic between the creation of God and the promise of God to man? I would rather spend my time doing the work of God among men, and doing it out in the marketplace as he did. Life has enough pain and disillusionment without fabricating conflicts and making these conflicts essential to the realization of God. This, I believe, is the fallacy of traditional religion: it ignores the gifts of God, the psalmist's joys, and substitutes a make-believe world. I, for one, see God in his creation.

3. DOES THE WORLD NEED
   SALVATION?

§ *YES*

Salvation is a restoring of life, and the world is slowly dying. It has abandoned God and has turned aside from the Church. Our civilization is hovering on the brink of nuclear holocaust. There seems to be no doubt that the world is sick. Our generation has seen more war than any previous generation, and the end is not in sight.

Catholics especially have begun to show signs of the great malaise. Churches are emptying. Vocations are down and fewer priests are being ordained, and many are leaving the Church. Not only is the world sick, but the very group that was commissioned by God to save the world from its sins is tottering. People have nowhere to turn.

Ours is a pampered, sick, and greedy generation. Violence seems to be the order of the day. Our universities, once citadels of learning and reason, are being turned into battlefields by the students. It's not safe to walk the streets at night; the crime rate is fantastic.

I don't fear the trials of this life, but I do fear that our children may never enter heaven because no one wants to teach them the right way. Parents stand in awe of their children and let them have their own way. If religion goes, then Christ's crucifixion will have been in vain; God is suffering, Our Lady is weeping, and the children of redemption have turned to false idols. I dread to think of the horrible nightmares that are in store for us if something doesn't bring us to our senses. Now they tell us that God is dead. The Supreme Court has taken God out of the schools, an action that is just a symptom of our godless society. Today we reap the horrible consequences.

❄ NO

The world does not need salvation, if by salvation you mean some magical, mysterious never-never land. The world does need help, but of a very earthly variety, not empty promises of eternal bliss from the pulpits. Its call for help needs to be answered; this will be its salvation. Its pains are not the traditional ones of sin and damnation. Its pains are the anguish and hunger of a humanity devoid of real leadership and inspiration. Christ told us we should not give a stone to a man who asked for bread. But how often hearts of stone deprive the hungry and the poor of bread!

The Catholic Church needs salvation. The Church has to

become human, which means divesting itself of pomp and circumstance. For too long it has ignored the miseries of the world. Now the world is surpassing the Church in its intellectual skill and expertise. The world is gaining back the people who fled it to search for God in monasteries and convents. Now they search for him in the taverns, in the go-go joints, in the hippie love-ins. "For wherever two or three are gathered together in my name, there I am in the midst of them." The world needs the salvation of the Church. Once the Church is saved, God will be returned to the masses.

4. DO YOU FAVOR A SCIENTIFIC APPROACH TO THE WORLD AND ITS PROBLEMS?

§ NO

If I understand it correctly, the concept of a scientific methodology is rather an exclusive one. It proposes itself to an *a priori* method, in which one accepts as certain a body of principles that are true in themselves. For example, two and two are four, or the whole is equal to the sum of its parts. A scientific method begins from a hypothesis, which necessarily must be demonstrated.

This scientific method is useful within a specific sphere, but in the realm of man and his understanding of God and his neighbor it is invalid. Throughout history man has built up a body of knowledge that he cannot reject, and for him to reject this patrimony would be tantamount to throwing the baby out with the bath water. In matters that pertain to religion and ethics, a man needs certitude if he is to make conclusions. A world of hypotheses would give rise to a sea of hypotheses, and we could never be certain of anything. Such an approach to the vital realms of God, the world, and man would spell sheer disaster. Aside from the disturbing doubts that would arise, there would be disagreement from every side. One man could make an observation and there would be no objective criterion of truth against which to measure it. Intellectual chaos would result. It is for these reasons that God endowed man with the ability to work out principles, principles that represent safe and sure starting points. A world of doubt and indecision cannot be a way of life. Truth needs reflection, and it is only when truth is found that man can follow a responsible pattern of action.

A prime virtue of the Catholic religion is its bank of certitude. There is no question about what is wrong and what is right. The Church's philosophy has served its theology well, so that its ethics are sure guides for the sincere person seeking to serve his God.

Many converts to the Catholic Church have marveled at the inner peace and security that arise from a devout and honest approach to Catholicism. What many objected to in their former religion was the elusiveness and transient quality of its dogma. One day they would hear one explanation of a particular doctrine, and on the next another explanation might emerge. This does not happen within the Catholic Church. Truth is truth be it in Korea, France, or the United States.

Principles also provide a solid base from which to approach the various problems of life. If we spend our life searching for truth, we do a good thing. If we spend our life serving the truth, we accomplish even more. The doubting approach may provide satisfaction in the laboratory, but it hardly answers the needs of man's day-to-day existence.

✳ YES

The scientific method is opposed to the dogmatic method. The dogmatic method arises from a body of principles held to be true. The fallacy of the dogmatic method arises from the belief that truth is something static and absolute. Actually, truth is relative and dynamic, and what is true today may not be true tomorrow. We once thought that the world was flat. We once felt that eating meat on Friday was a mortal sin, but we reject that idea today. We once thought that war could be justified. Many reject this today.

The more man matures intellectually, the more sophisticated he becomes. He may hesitate to accept as certain a premise that he accepted at one time, because a maturing intellect detects more and more facets in any given situation. A maturing intellect rejects the static as deadening. The scientific method turns periods into question marks. It accepts few dicta and tries to find its own reasons for reality. Once a man accepts truth as static, he finds no more function for his intellect other than repeating the kernels of truth he thinks he has acquired. It is then that life passes him by.

Pope John XXIII emphasized that religion should be less dogmatic and more vital, that it benefits more from a merciful, understanding approach to life than from a cold, doctrinal approach. Theologians have always been afraid that anything but a dogmatic approach to God would be self-defeating. Religion benefits from the scientific method, because it weeds out trivia and enforces a healthy rigorism and a demanding pattern of thought. For example, the scientific method of hypothesis accepts as true only that which is evidenced as true through specific patterns of trial, error, and searching. The same methods that have brought progress in medicine, industry, and other fields have since shown what advantages they can bring to religion and ethics.

The scientific method makes religion more understandable to man and develops a body of thought that is appealing because it is human and rational. If the scientific method did nothing else but prune the excess foliage in our concepts of God, man, and the world, its use would be justified.

Principles should never become gods, nor should they block intellectual growth. The history of man has not yet been written definitively, nor has the path of man toward God and neighbor become so clear that man need not continue to search for it. Truth will always be elusive, and the search for it not only makes man more careful and more attentive, but it also forces him to respect each fleeting contact he makes with it. Francis Thompson in his poem *The Hound of Heaven* not only depicts man's search for God, but also the rushing vitality and excitement that is possible when man remains man and does not succumb to the temptation to play God.

5. ARE YOU PROUD OF THE HISTORY OF THE CATHOLIC CHURCH?

§ *YES*

The history of the Church is fascinating and inspiring. A Church that has withstood so much and yet is still able to carry the torch of faith is worth our reverent pride. The Crusades, for instance, were one of the most triumphant eras in the history of the Church. So much suffering and heroism are written into this period. The words of Christ that Christians should go out and preach the Gospel to every creature were given meaning.

Who cannot take pride in the accomplishments of the Church in science, literature, and education? The monks were the custodians of culture, and they added their own contributions. The Augustines and the Aquinases strongly affect our lives today. The Doctors of the Church were masters of literature and pedagogy. Then there were the great Cardinals Richelieu and Newman, and the layman Thomas More, all of whom contributed immensely toward the growth of the Church.

We have every reason to be proud of what the Church has accomplished. Rather than seeking to disassociate ourselves from our past as the new radicals suggest, we should seek to live up to our traditions and maintain the continuity of distinction and superiority associated with our faith.

The Catholic Church started out simply, a band of fishermen. Today it is a mighty force for good. The contribution of Catholicism to culture and science, its moral leadership down through the centuries, all of this bespeaks the presence and inspiration of Jesus Christ. Even when the gates of hell threatened, the Church rose to the occasion. Picture the frail figure of Pope Leo facing Attila the Hun, or the ascetic Pius standing firm against Hitler, and you know you are part of something great.

Whether you agree with all that history tells us about the Church or not, you cannot read its pages without sensing the magnificence of Catholicism. Our culture owes the Church a huge debt. But more important than that, we in the twentieth century should draw inspiration from our history, we should be proud to be associated with the one true Church, for in all of history it has shown itself the able and reliable defender of the one true God and his creation, mankind.

✳ NO

An archbishop once stated that the Catholic Church has been in the forefront of civil rights since 1919. A black person in the audience was heard to remark that if what we have today represents the progress achieved by that leadership, we might as well give up now. Christianity looks out today upon a world that is composed largely of people who are poor and hungry.

Catholicism set itself apart from the rest of humanity as the savior of mankind. Its accomplishments, realistically speaking, are hardly outstanding. We have many things we can be proud of in our history, but there are also many things about which we can be ashamed—the Inquisition, the suppression of Galileo, the religious wars and, yes, the Crusades. I hate to think of how many people have suffered mental and physical anguish at the hands of Christians. Six million Jews were put to death by Christians. I think of the little children and the helpless women in Nazi Germany whose only crime was that they were not Christians.

When one visits Rome, he wonders about the riches of the Church and the poverty of the world. Was not the French Revolution an uprising against the Catholic rulers of those times? Why did Pope Pius not speak out against the Nazis, and why was it more a sin to be a communist than a fascist or a Nazi? Why was Franco given so much patronizing attention, and why are the dictatorships of South America so closely allied with the Church? Why was Thomas Aquinas persecuted for injecting the thoughts of the pagan Aristotle into Christian doctrine? Why was dissent condemned, and fawning, obsequious flattery encouraged?

Where is truth in Catholic history? Where is the dignity of the human person? Why were men forced to endure gargantuan humiliations when they dared point out the weakness of a Church grown too complacent and un-Christian? I think of the persecution of scientists and the divorce of reason from faith. I look at the majestic cathedrals and the opulence of the papal court and wonder if Christ would ever feel at home in such splendor. The Roman Curia even today has the power to make a brilliant writer or scientist *persona non grata*.

Absolute power has corrupted the Church just as it has corrupted nations. The Church has survived only because God raised up great reformers and leaders who were not tainted by the foul air of clericalism, men such as Francis of Assisi, Isaac Hecker, Teilhard de Chardin, John XXIII. Our apologetic texts have written off the horrors of the Inquisition and make light of the Galileo persecution. The Church may alter the writings of history and blur those things that might throw a shadow over its past, but men today are more discerning. Our sense of values has matured. We judge a reality by its accomplishments! What has it produced, how has it contributed to the total good of mankind?

Once the incense of self-adulation has cleared away and the bright lights of medieval liturgies have been extinguished, the Church must stand on its record. Catholicism has not succeeded, and its accomplishments do not measure up to the commands of Christ. To feed the hungry, to clothe the naked, to bring peace on earth, to become poor in spirit, meek, gentle, this is what Christ founded his Church to do. The record shows much left to be done, despite the gifts of time and opportunity given the Church.

In our day, we are finally untangling the nonessentials from the core of the Christian vocation. We are turning from the ritualistic and striving to embrace the richer dimensions of human fulfillment written into the Christian message. Much remains to be done. We can look to history to help us avoid the mistakes of our forebears. We cannot condemn those who went before us, however. They practiced religion and followed the Gospel as they understood it. Our mistake would be to write them off. Another mistake would be to see history as a laurel wreath instead of a prod. We do not have time to engage in polemics or panegyrics about the past. We can only move forward so that history's mistakes may not be our own.

I favor a study of history, then, to arm the Christian. But I see history only as a teacher, a stern teacher, warning us to stay closer to the Gospel.

6. IS IT EVER RIGHT TO TELL A LIE?

§ NO

A lie is intrinsically evil. It violates the very nature of man and therefore degrades him and all he touches. A lie is despicable, and under no circumstances can it be tolerated. The father of lies is Satan, and his lie to God and our first parents caused the horrible evils that beset us—war, sin, injustice, and death.

St. Thomas tells us every lie is a sin, and it is extenuating circumstances that can reduce it to a venial sin. St. Thomas considers it unnatural and unjust to express other than what one has in his mind. A lie is contrary to the very nature of God, who is the way and the truth. Because of their unnaturalness, lies are forbidden by the Eighth Commandment. The Old Testament states repeatedly that lying is hateful to the Lord, and St. John in the Apocalypse (21:8; 22:16) reminds us that liars who are unrepentant will suffer the eternal torments of hell.

Today people speak about a credibility gap, which only shows us how contradictory the world is becoming. It is all right to lie and cheat in business, but when the government withholds information, which is its right, then we say that the President is a liar. We are beginning to see a world where truth is a rarity and lying a mode of life. Some people accuse the bishops and the Church in general of lying, when all they are doing is defending the truth. People refuse to accept the truth, especially when it makes demands on their consciences.

What about mental reservation? Is that a lie? We understand a lie to be what St. Augustine describes as a method of speaking that contradicts the intention of the speaker, but a mental reservation does not contradict the intention.

Suppose a salesman calls at your home, and you do not care

to see him. You tell one of your children to inform the salesman you are not home. Is this a sin? Moral theology tells us that mental reservation is not a lie, since you do not have the intention to deceive, first of all, and you are reserving the thought that you are not at home to this salesman. In common custom, it is accepted that when you do not care to see someone, you simply state that you are not at home, meaning "to this particular person." In the same way, we are not guilty of lying when we do not tell a sick person that he has cancer, lest the shock be too great for him. We are really avoiding a greater evil.

Although the intention to deceive is not substantially part of a lie, deception is ordinarily considered as lying, for it is hiding the truth. When there is no reason to justify withholding the truth, then a person is considered a liar. There is much being written today to weaken the theology that condemns lying. People are finding new definitions and wider loopholes. But no one can get away from the fundamental reality that a lie contradicts the truth, and as such violates God, who is truth.

The Church has always stood for the truth, and its sons and daughters have died to preserve it. At no time has the Church aligned itself for personal motives with those who live the big lie. It not only teaches the truth, but lives it, and this is the best example it can give to those of us who are beset on all sides with purveyors of falsehood and evil.

❈ YES

The Church has contradicted itself for many centuries in its theology of lying. The mental reservation is sheer casuistry and fools no one. The Church made the lie seem so heinous on the one hand and then on the other has found loopholes to justify what pure common sense says is allowable. If I don't want to tell a person something, I cannot be forced into doing so. We cannot conclude that everyone has the right to know everything. Merely because someone puts a question to me does not thereby give that person the right to know the answer. Such a view is simplistic and basically illogical. It has been responsible for a lot of unnecessary hardship and pain.

Now theologians are beginning to view the concept of lying from a more realistic and sensible point of view. By that I mean that emphasis is placed on whether or not the person asking a question has a right to know the answer. For example, a priest or a doctor could be asked to reveal a private matter and might decline to answer by stating that the person asking does not have the right to know the answer. Although it will be argued that all persons have the right to know the truth, it must also be kept in mind that a person's right has to be governed by the demands of the common good. If privileged information were available to any and all persons, irreparable harm would come to the individuals concerned.

The Church has to place less emphasis on the heinousness of lying and more on the positive aspect of truth itself. Truth can help man understand his own transcendence. It can open up a refreshing, fulfilling world to him. The search for truth is as exhilarating as the possession of it. Truth is reality, expressing itself in all its completeness, and spurring man on to a greater awareness of his own role in the plan of creation. The Church has to offer man a path to truth that is less negative than present doctrine, one that will help man find the Christ who said he was the way and the truth. Theology that is devoted to discovering ways of circumventing the law rather than opening up the riches of the world is a decaying force. It is man's need to trust his fellow man, to believe in him, and to receive support from the Church in this quest. When the Church recognizes its role in the unveiling of truth in all its aspects, then it will become the living symbol of Christ.

7. DO YOU THINK THE RIGHT OF PRIVATE PROPERTY IS SUPREME?

§ YES

Private property is a moral right, even though some people deny this. Communists, especially, are against the right of private property because they consider property owners as exploiters of the people. Pope Leo XIII declared that the destruction of private property robs the lawful possessor of what is his just due and brings the state into a sphere that is not its own. In his encyclical *Quadragesimo anno*, Pope Pius XI vindicated the right of private property once and for all.

Some argue that because there are evils in the capitalistic system one must therefore abandon it. No one denies evils in this system, such as enslavement of the poor, control of governments, manipulation of the press, and so on. But one does not cure a disease by killing the patient. Once you deny the right to private property, you open the door for socialism and communism, both of which are atheistic and inhuman.

In many Western countries we see programs that take away the initiative of the individual and the rewards of private enterprise. Socialism tends to destroy incentive and encourage leeches.

If people were encouraged to respect private property, private industry, and individual initiative, the evils of capitalism would hardly exist. Man is ordained to earn his bread by the sweat of his brow. St. Paul tells us that if a man does not work, he should not eat. Private property as a goal encourages enterprise. In the Catholic religion we are taught that the right of private property is a moral right, based on human nature. Not only individuals have a right to private property, but corporations, families, and even the Church. When God put man on earth, he gave him the right to the possession of his own goods, the right to enjoy the fruits of his labor.

The Catholic Church considers labor as a means to an end. Private ownership demands stewardship, meaning that the right has limitations. Public authority has the duty to enforce a wise and prudent use of private property, but it never has a right to take away that property or its use without just indemnification. The rights and limitations of private property give mankind an insight into God's plan for man. We are able to understand why God created us, and marvel at how he provides for the stability and progress of the individual.

✳ NO

A writer in the early Church said that since the earth and the fullness thereof belong to the Lord, it is correct to assume that our possessions are the gifts of the Lord and so belong also to our fellow man. I am not advocating communism or a welfare state. But I think the concept of private property has been abused to the point that human life is placed below the right to property. Not only has the right of private property been extended to justify wanton disregard of the right to life and human dignity, but today it is used as a subtle device to justify discrimination. This is obviously the case with those who object to open-housing legislation. My house is my house and my kingdom, so I can sell or refuse to sell to whomever I please, goes the ploy. Cardinal McIntyre, the aged conservative of California, showed the "Christian" world how to make best use of this basic human right in order to prevent other human beings from enjoying human dignity. People speak of the limitations of a right, but seldom care to speculate on the consequences of the limitations.

We all know that the common good regulates all our human rights, and that rights entail duties. Leo XIII in his encyclical *Rerum novarum* stated that whenever the general interest or any particular class suffers or is threatened with injury that can in no other way be met or prevented, it is the duty of the public authority to intervene. Private-property supremacists forget that this is what happens when two-thirds of the world goes to bed hungry every night: a particular class is threatened. Those of us who are blessed with the good things of this earth must be sensitive to the needs of those who lack them. We may object to the excessive demands made on our resources, but we cannot write off the people who are helped by the government to a more dignified plateau in life. No one has the right merely to do what he wants with his property. Rather, he must practice responsible stewardship.

The communists exaggerate when they pretend to war against private ownership. They place an overemphasis on the worker in order to correct an imbalance whereby much wealth is concentrated in the hands of a few. Their method falls short of its goal, because they reject private initiative and human dignity. We are in a sorry state, however, when religious leaders can play one political system against the other, and not only confuse people but even damage them and their sense of values.

What our religion needs is a greater understanding of man's social obligations and a sharper realization of the delicate balance existing between man's rights and duties.

8. DO YOU BELIEVE IN THE CONCEPT OF GRACE?

§ YES

Today you hear very little about grace. Only a few years ago people sought grace and stressed its importance, but today no one seems to care much about it. Long ago, Pelagius taught that man by his own efforts alone could achieve salvation. The Council of Trent condemned Pelagius as a heretic. Why? Because he made God superfluous, and attributed to man powers that are not properly his. Pelagius thought very little of grace, and we seem to be falling into the same error in our own time.

Grace is the life of God in man. Grace enables us to perform acts that can be rewarded by our heavenly Father. Actual grace is the assistance that God offers to man; sanctifying grace is the spiritual health and glory of a soul that is not in sin.

Some people believe that the concept of grace detracts from the dignity of man. How can the assistance of God, who is our Creator, in any way have a deleterious effect on man? The Church has always defended the dignity of mankind and the power of reason against those who would reduce man to a spiritual automaton. But it has ever been alert to defend the rights of God over man. Grace is God's gift to man whereby man is enabled to act in a way that is above his natural powers. Grace elevates man and enhances his nature. We are able to enjoy the life of grace through the merits of Christ's passion and death. Christ attained for mankind the possibility of a supernatural life, and if he had not died for us and redeemed us, we would have remained slaves of Satan.

We do not realize how much we need this help of God. St. Paul taught that grace was necessary merely to have salutary thoughts, purposes, and performance. We need actual grace so that we may be strengthened in our hours of temptation, and through sanctifying grace we are kept from sin. The Church teaches us that we are temples of the Holy Spirit and that through sanctifying grace we share in the divine life and become adopted sons of God.

Grace, then, forms a vital part of the Catholic way of life. All that we are and all that we do stems from our association with God, achieved through the sacrament of baptism and fostered through a life of prayer and sacramental grace. The man who lives the life of grace is assured that if he works his salvation in fear and trembling, if he chastises his body and brings it into subjection, then God will be with him in his hour of judgment. No one can be sure that he will receive the gift of final perseverance. But he can be sure that God will not abandon his faithful ones and that if he truly follows Christ, then he can achieve a glorious reunion with Christ in eternity.

✻   NO

The term "grace" is rather meaningless. Some may accuse me of Pelagianism for saying this, but what consequence does this label have? The problem is really one of semantics. I love God, and I choose freely to follow the example of Christ as revealed in man's nature and in the historical traditions of the evangelists. If grace has any meaning, it is a relationship with God through which I can communicate with him and he communicates with me. Grace shows me God's mercy, and I see this mercy as something that God freely offers me. But I do not like to view grace as a spiritual quality of the soul, as if grace offered nothing to me as a person, body and soul. I do not like the idea that God constantly has to be giving me shots in the arm, to keep me thinking about him, loving him, and working for him. I follow Christ and I search for him, but I feel I can be trusted to follow through on my commitment. I think the former concept of grace takes away man's responsibility. It removes too much of man's freedom under the guise of helping him.

One must ask himself that if the power for good comes from God, and if the sustaining of a person in his motivation also comes from God, then is it not God who is performing the action? The need for a concept of grace is consequent upon the separation of man's life into the natural and the supernatural. If you explain the supernatural as a sphere above man's nature, then you have to set up a fictional power—in this instance, grace—through which he can exist in that sphere. The concept of grace is also necessary if one thinks of his God-relationship in a purely vertical sense, as a God-me relationship. Once you expand your concept of man and his basic God-consciousness, you do not need to create esoteric powers for him. If man is God's creature initially, and if he is equipped by nature with intelligence and freedom, he will follow God if he wants to do so.

It is here that an expanded view of man's powers can be seen. If man is in the service of God, he acts on behalf of the kingdom of God because he sees need. In other words, the stimulus for action is in his environment. He helps his neighbor because he freely chooses to follow his life's option. You don't have to complicate man's religious activity with notions of divine infusions like grace. Man is responsible for his good actions and his bad actions. He acts as a free agent. He acts because he wants to act, because he sees need, and because he realizes that the help he gives his neighbor redounds to his own fulfillment.

Grace gives true power when seen simply as a communicating relationship with God, based on understanding of self, neighbor, and world.

IV

THE
CATHOLIC
CHURCH
AND
RELIGION

Most people belong to some kind of church. To some it's like a club where they meet friends and think about ways of pleasing God. Others belong to a church only in name, and seldom make an appearance at religious functions. They help support their church and lend their names to it, but more than that they will not do. What they fear most may be the interference of the religious leaders in their personal lives. Then there are many good people who belong to no religion at all. They look upon organized religion as anathema, claiming that it hampers their freedom of movement and constitutes an obstacle between them and God.

We have to admit that belonging to a church, either nominally or wholeheartedly, does give us a certain status. At least, it makes us feel that we are dedicated in some way to Christian principles. Also, church membership puts us in a special category. People think of us as God-fearing and good. They might even think we are pillars of the church if we support the church through faithful attendance and regular contributions.

People, then, are usually pressured morally or socially to join a church. It makes them feel safe and even good. It makes others look up to them. They attain a feeling of security about their future beyond the grave.

Why did you choose your particular religion? Are you satisfied with it? Did you ever think of changing to another religion? Or, perhaps, have you ever been tempted to abandon it altogether? If so, why didn't you do it?

Many great men were not members of an organized religion. Voltaire once said that he loved himself and he loved God, but he couldn't stand the people who got in the way of himself and God. Other great men formed their own religions, not finding in the existing creeds anything to satisfy their needs. Still others took an existing religion and completely transformed it. For their labors these men have been given a firm place in history.

If you are a member of the Catholic religion, you find yourself in one of the most tightly organized churches in the world. More than that, it is a religion that openly labels itself as the only true religion founded by Christ himself. It teaches that all other religions are shams, even though the people belonging to them are in good faith.

In this chapter we would like to explore possible concepts of religion in general, without necessarily stressing Catholicism. But we think you should consider seriously your belief in this faith. Why is religion even necessary? What are we to think of St. Paul's statement that there is only one intermediary between God and man, and that is Jesus? Does the Church make too many demands on a person, thereby hindering him from fulfilling his relationship with God? Who censors the censor? Are you willing at least to examine these questions?

1. IS THE PRESENT SITUATION IN THE CHURCH CHAOTIC?

§ YES

Definitely. The moral fiber of most Catholics shows signs of wear and tear. Leadership is lacking on all major issues, not because of a leadership lag, but because people are rejecting the leadership.

Pope Paul is said to have shed bitter tears recently, lashing out at those who would hurt the renewal in the Church and prostitute the rich heritage of Pope John XXIII.

The confusion is reflected in widespread disillusionment. People feel betrayed. Leaders without any sense of tradition are trying to take over, and they are forcing the good people to leave the Church in droves.

Disobedience is the "in" thing. Even priests and nuns disobey. People are being encouraged to follow their consciences, and no one pays any attention to the Pope any more. Everything sacred is mocked and reviled.

False prophets abound, and the Bible is laughed at. It seems that the anti-Christ is upon us. These are dark days. Everything is upside down. Yes, it almost seems these are the latter days when even the elect are deceived.

Basic dogmas, even the Eucharist, the Blessed Sacrament, are questioned. Anyone with a table seems able to start his own Mass. Conversions are down. The Church is losing its moral power over men. And the sad thing is that the erosion comes from within.

✳ NO

It all depends on what you mean by chaos. How helpless does a little updating, long overdue, make you? The situation in the Church is far from chaotic, if by "chaotic" you mean self-destructive.

Catholics are experiencing growing pains. Rather than simply wringing his hands and wailing, one should search out the causes of the confusion. He should be mature enough to cope with dissent. He could emerge from it stronger and more deeply committed.

The confusion in the Church is symptomatic of the need for reform. The Church has let things go to seed. Excitement, movement, and evolution are healthy signs. They reveal tension, a springing away from all unhealthy, frozen forms. The past forms of the Church are certainly not eternal.

Why decry the signs of rebirth in the Catholic Church? Why pine after the good old days? It is more realistic to determine the direction of this new impetus and position oneself to gain the most from it: to take advantage of the dynamism to propel oneself forward.

What is disturbing in all this confusion is the alarming number of confused people. Leaders especially are abdicating their role. If the leaders are confused, then the creative person must move ahead on his own, for he has intelligence and freedom, and a destiny to fulfill. His conscience must guide him toward resourceful action.

2. IS RELIGION THE OPIATE OF THE PEOPLE?

§ NO

Karl Marx called religion the opiate of the people, and his loyal followers have proven how much they believe this to be true. Basically, communism is atheistic. Communists naturally hate religion, since religion points up the basic fallacy of communism: that the value of a person is based on the amount of work he can do. Exploiting the working class as they do, destroying all class lines in society, the communists have no room for a God-concept.

Christianity tells us that God exists and that he must be worshiped, that we must help mankind and not keep it in bondage. You will not find any slave-labor camps in Christian countries, but you will find men loving one another and trying to help alleviate the misery and pain to which so many poor people are heir.

In removing God from their lives, the communists lose their love for man. They put the blame for the world's troubles at the door of religion because they seek a scapegoat, and at the same time they want to remove man's basic identification with a God-figure. This makes it easier for them to set up their own rules and distort society. Naturally, believing in their atheistic philosophy, the communists attack religion, for religion is the sole remaining bastion of truth and justice for all mankind. Nothing in reality drugs men's minds more and causes them to act irrationally and unjustly than the materialistic and antihuman philosophy of communism.

✳ YES

Karl Marx did call religion the opiate of the people, but because I agree that it can become an opiate doesn't mean I am a communist. On the contrary, I believe in the dignity of the human being and the responsibility of one human being toward another, based on the brotherhood of man. I don't believe in exploiting the masses, nor do I think a classless society is feasible. I am not atheistic, nor do I subscribe to the inhuman methods attributed to the Leninists and Stalinists.

Organized religion can become an opiate when it destroys initiative and spontaneous Christian response. A church that merely provides a list of laws and oral responses and leads its people as though they were cattle provides nothing more than a flight from reality. It induces an unreal attitude toward life, a kind of souped-up euphoria. Religious leaders sometimes use religion to force the masses to respond in a predetermined and selfish way, as witness the "gas station" services that substitute for real religion in so many Catholic churches on Sunday morning. People rush into Mass, pay no attention, and put up with boring ritual simply to satisfy a conditioned need. Religion that produces such drugged responses hurts the total person, and is truly an opiate.

3. DOES RELIGION HAVE TO BE LINKED TO AN ORGANIZED CHURCH?

§ YES

Religion must be connected with an organized church. Religion represents a set of beliefs, for example, the Apostles' Creed. How can one put these beliefs into practice without drawing people with similar beliefs into some form of organization? How would one protect the purity and substance of these beliefs without setting up an organization?

Man's social nature is fulfilled through membership in clubs and societies. Like any organization, a religion needs leaders to study and perfect the basic creed so that all are able to share the results of research and diligent study. I find it hard to imagine people with similar beliefs and hopes not banding together into some kind of organization, simply to share their insights and to put their creed into practice.

People who fight the organized Church and seek to destroy it really want to set up their own organization with their own rules and regulations. What is happening today in the rebellion against religion is a resentment against all authority.

An organization protects the individual and makes it possible for people with the same beliefs to operate as a unit, thereby making a greater impact on their environment. No one person can do as much as a collective force. People can criticize the organized Church as much as they want, but they cannot come up with an adequate substitute. Ultimately any group has to become selective in its membership, otherwise it winds up with anarchy. It has to set up rules and regulations, and thereby limit the freedom of its membership. This is true especially in the Catholic religion, which admits of few gray areas. Either you believe or you don't. It's that simple.

❋ NO

I don't think that religion and the organized Church must necessarily be linked. History shows us that some of the greatest Christians refused to be shackled by a group mentality. Religion is an expression of the soul. It is our response to God's love for us. We hear what he did for us, we are grateful for it, so we want to do something for him. We want to help others. I think the best expression of religion is the golden rule.

Most people resent that organized religion is a product of another century and another mentality. It is not contemporary. Its crippling list of "dos" and "don'ts" might have been all right in a less enlightened age, but today simply reflect a lack of trust in the individual's integrity. Organized religion tends to get bogged down in its own problems and forget why it was founded. Eventually it scarcely reflects the personal responses of individuals as it tries to force prefabricated beliefs and trappings on its members.

The Catholic religion is the best example of this. Young children are brainwashed into believing the most impossible fantasies, and their spontaneity and freshness suffer. One year it is a sin to eat meat on Friday; the next year it makes no difference. Old men in the Church pass on their fears and guilts to succeeding generations.

Although I think we need to group together, religion should exhibit the contemporaneousness, freshness, and vitality that spring from man himself.

4. IS THE CONCEPT OF ONE TRUE RELIGION REALISTIC?

§ YES

The Church teaches us that there can be only one true religion, and this is the Catholic religion. All other Christian religions were founded out of the discontent and rebellion of men. The Catholic religion was founded by Christ. Truth cannot be found in all the religions existing today. Religion is supposed to bring spiritual peace to a person, but too many religions simply confuse.

Religions cannot teach contradictions. One religion says it's all right to divorce, and another says that divorce is evil. For guidance we have to go to the Bible, which is the word of God. The Catholic Church stands the test of the Bible, because its teachings spring from it. If God is truth, and if religion is a response to God's love and mercy, then how can we have anything but one true religion? To say otherwise is to mock God's truth.

I wouldn't know which religion to choose if there were not some external signs to help me decide. I find in the Gospel that Christ came to unify, to make one. He came to put all men under his protection. He is our shepherd, and I will follow in his fold. I prefer to stick with the religion he started than join one of the groups founded by malcontents. With Christ I can be sure, because he is God.

✻ NO

I honestly cannot see how the concept of one true religion is a realistic one. I think that any religion that is real religion is true. I think that you can have as many religions as you can have sincere, honest, and dedicated people. Religion is true when it understands God and his creation. Religion is true when it makes one want to heed the word of God found in one's own heart. I don't see religion in candlesticks and incense, cathedrals and scarlet robes, all of which distort Christ's original intention. I say the Apostles' Creed, but I cannot see this simple cataloguing of beliefs and ritual resembling medieval court pageantry as fulfilling the definition of religion.

The Catholic Church especially claims to have been founded by Christ. But Christ did not found the Vatican, nor did he live and die to give his name to lavish chancery buildings and soaring Gothic architecture. I think religion is enshrined in the blood and sweat of man's being. We get hung up on organized religion as an inheritance, making of it a golden calf, whereas religion should be man's personal path to God and his fellow man. However a man wants to express his love of God seems true to me. And I'm sure it's true to God.

Service to God and neighbor is the best religious service: "As long as you did it unto the least of my brethren, you did it unto me." I don't think anyone can equate membership in only one organization with God's will: "All men shall know you are my disciples if you have love one for another." One cannot dictate love's expression, nor can he force it. Religion is a one-to-one relationship between a man and God. How can anyone possibly tell me that attendance in a brick and mortar palace, with organ music in the dimly lit interior, is a substitute for an individual's intimate expression of his gratitude for life, God, and selfhood? There can be as many religions as there are creatures made in the image and likeness of God.

5. HAS RELIGION EXERCISED PROPER MORAL LEADERSHIP?

§ YES

Organized religion has come under heavy attack from irresponsible critics. Upset because they cannot have their own way, they put the blame for society's ills on organized religion. This is childish and unjust. Actually, such criticism barely hides a desire to do away with organized religion, and as such it is diabolical.

Christianity has always tried to bring out the best in man's nature. It has always exerted the most intense effort to help man achieve the God-like potential that is in him. The leaders of our major religious faiths cannot be held responsible for individual failures to fulfill the challenge of their teachings. It is true that organized religion has made mistakes in the past, but this only proves that it is human. It is a frail instrument of the divine.

Organized religion, however, not only admits its mistakes, but it is doing something about them. Vatican II is the best sign of the good faith and hope among the hierarchy of the Catholic Church. Pope John and Pope Paul have both admitted the failings of the Church. But it is one thing to make mistakes, and quite another thing to let oneself become a scapegoat. The bitter accusations hurled against Pope Pius XII on the Nazi question are not only untrue, but senseless. Our society owes much to the leadership of men like Pius XII. Modern civilization, in fact, would not have been able to advance to the degree it has without the support and understanding of our major religions. Moral leadership was exercised in leading men to appreciate their worth and thus fulfill their potential.

I fail to see why organized religion should stand indicted because of a few minor failings. This is vicious and cruel, and shameless ingratitude. Let us join hands to help the major religions, rather than point accusing fingers.

✳ NO

Organized religion has a grave responsibility to exercise leadership. I think of the words of Gandhi: "I love your Christ, but I hate your Christians." I think of the accusations that the Catholic religion is a white racist society, made not by irresponsible critics but by sincere black priests. I think of the thousands of innocent people who are killed in Vietnam, representing in many cases Christian fighting Christian. I think of the sincere religions that are subjected to inhuman indignities and injustices in the name of Christianity. I think of the billions of Chinese and Indians who are pariahs to the Christian, and who are left to writhe in hunger and misery because of political or religious indifference. I think of the squalor of so many Southern Negro communities, where whites and blacks separate even at the communion rail.

I think of Pope Paul crying, "War, never more war," and of a cardinal saying, "My country, right or wrong." I think of an archbishop pleading for a return to the recitation of the rosary and ignoring the smug complacency of his indifferent, racist, white flock. I think of the unwillingness of so many religious communities to abandon their white fortresses and set up a meaningful religious life in the ghettos and poverty areas of our country.

Where is the world going and what is its future? What kind of answers is organized religion giving to a civilization that encompasses the richest hope and the blackest despair? I honestly feel that the best answer organized religion could give is to reorganize.

6. ISN'T THE EXISTENCE OF SO MANY CHRISTIAN RELIGIONS AN ARGUMENT AGAINST RELIGION ITSELF?

§ NO

Many people have said that the scandal of Christendom is the proliferation of denominations. Pope John called Vatican II in an effort to unite the whole of Christendom. He spoke sadly of the tear in the seamless robe of Christ. He tried to unite Christendom through his own personal kindness and warm personality.

To decry the scandal of a divided Christendom is one thing, but to conclude that therefore religion itself is wrong and useless is silly. I don't see how anyone can hope to eradicate organized religion and still expect to effect any real transformation of the world. I don't believe that one religion is as good as another. And I'm not convinced that all religions were founded in good faith. But I look upon the existence of so many religions as an expression of man's basic desire to conform to God's will. At the same time, since we Catholics possess the one true religion, I think that we should work in a true spirit of brotherhood to lead the stray sheep back to the fold.

I am all for the ecumenical movement, so long as it doesn't mean that we water down our basic dogmas or give up our principal belief, that Christ founded only one Church. Protestants and Jews are good people, but they are misguided. They do not have the truth. But this is not their fault. I think we have to sit down with non-Catholics and discuss the truth with them in a patient yet firm dialogue.

Religion is here to stay. Christ founded only one true Church, and that is built on the rock of Peter: "You are Peter and upon this rock I will build my Church, and the gates of hell shall not prevail against it." Thus I see the ecumenical movement as a moving toward Rome, and I expect that ultimately other religions will see the folly of their ways and return to their Father's home, which is Catholicism.

❋ YES

I cannot see how people refuse to accept the fact that organized religion is basically an expression of the individual's desire to serve Christ. And therefore I cannot see how one can justify the hundreds of splinter groups that call themselves legitimate religions. The notion of religion demands unity, at least that is what the proponents of organized religion tell us. How can we look with favor upon the various religious bodies as expressions of Christian love and truth when they fail to agree upon basic principles, when they manifest an uncharitable and unedifying disunity?

I have heard that in mission territories, rivalries and even meanness arise between denominational groups. A Catholic priest will disparage and refuse to help a Seventh Day Adventist, spurning even the slightest attempt at cooperation. If this is religion, who wants any part of it? I think the splinter groups have built a Tower of Babel, with one message coming from one side and a contradictory one from the other.

Organized religion frequently does not express the love and charity of Christ. There is too much in-fighting and too much desire to save the institution, rather than to get busy doing the work of the Gospel. Young people are turning away from organized religion and seeking through drugs and rebellion the freedom to search out God.

I don't think the Catholic Church has the right idea about the ecumenical movement. It is compounding differences by standing firm on its dogmas. The Church is saying, Let's unite, so long as you all agree with us. This is childish. Let the bickering cease and the sincerity show through, and perhaps people will become convinced that there really is something to organized religion.

7. DO YOU THINK CATHOLICS NEGLECT THE BIBLE?

§   NO

The Bible has always been a very important part of the Catholic religion. It could not have been otherwise, since the Bible is a source of divine revelation. Catholics have always been accused of neglecting the Bible, and some even say that the Bible has been played down so that no one would read it. The inference of course is that the Bible is not found in Catholic homes and that it is given no more than lip service in Catholic doctrine.

Most Protestant sects have made the Bible the sole source of doctrine. We are all very familiar with the Bible-totin' preachers of the South, who can quote chapter and verse by memory and who spew forth fear of the Lord with every breath.

I must admit that many Catholics are not as familiar with the Bible as they should be. But this does not mean the Church itself neglects the Bible. Some of the best research on the Bible has been done by Catholic scholars. Catholics have always insisted that the Bible is inspired. In its liturgy the Church draws heavily upon the Bible, and priests are bound under pain of mortal sin to read portions of it daily in their breviary.

The Church rejects individual interpretation of the Bible. Because it teaches that the Bible is the inspired word of God, it will not tolerate mutilation of the Bible's meanings by individuals. The Church uses the Bible to support its teachings, and since the Pope is infallible, it would not make sense to have the infallible teachings of the Church contradicted by an individual who believes himself to have the right to his own interpretation of the Bible. This would produce chaos.

Protestants are great defenders of private interpretation, and as a result there are as many different religious sects as individual readers. With individual interpretation there is no guarantee that the divine inspiration will not be altered to suit a situation.

I am pained to hear of many so-called scholars who belittle the Bible and question the validity of the sacred books. I remember reading of a priest who taught that the Bible was mere history, and as such shared in the fallibility of any historical document. He tore down the book of Genesis especially, insisting that the Old Testament in general is filled with myth and folklore. He poked fun at the Christmas story, saying there is little credibility to be given the Magi and Infancy narratives.

The Bible has always been a source of strength and inspiration to the Catholic family, and although most of us were not dutiful in our study of the Old Testament, we have given the New Testament, and especially the Gospels, the reverential attention that the revealed word of God merits.

❊ *YES*

I think Catholics have neglected the Bible, since they have not made it the pattern for their actions. By that I mean more emphasis has been put on Tradition, or the historical revelation of our forebears. Tradition and the Bible have long been considered twin fonts of Catholic teachings. This despite the fact that divine revelation presumably is found in the inspired books of the Bible.

Say what you will, few Catholics feel at home with the Bible. Yet when one considers the New Testament, he finds this sense of strangeness difficult to understand, for the New Testament is purported to be the testimony of Christ's teaching and activity while on earth. The Church has given more emphasis to papal pronouncements and the lives of the saints than to the life of God in the Scriptures.

Biblical scholarship has not been the hallmark of the Catholic Church. The current interest in biblical studies in the Church is merely a bandwagon kind of revival. It is to the Protestant world of scholarship that we owe the concept of form criticism and the anthropological insights now accepted in Catholic circles. We can thank our Protestant brethren for advances in exegesis, hermeneutics, literary genre, and realistic biblical theology. Because of these, the Bible is no longer used simply to prop up Church teaching. We are beginning to sift the sentimental from the substantial in our doctrinal arsenal.

The second Vatican Council reminds us that although God speaks in sacred Scripture, he does so through men and, therefore, in human fashion. Catholics must take special pains to investigate the meanings of the sacred writers, leaving no stone unturned to discover what God wanted to manifest through their words. That means we have to pay special attention to the literary forms of the Bible, and also study the customs and expression current at the time of the writing. A discerning attitude must be adopted, lest we find conflict between the text and the reality that surrounds us.

Priests especially must recognize that the sacred writings are basically an expression of a particular culture; they are the author's responses to the reality of God. Bearing this in mind, the priest must open up the Scriptures to us in his preaching, but at the same time he must not overlook the fact that Christ is also speaking to us in our contemporary literature, for the word of God transcends time and makes itself heard in the idiom of our day.

A new era can open up for the Catholic Church if it is faithful to the divine writings and to the realization that God chooses men to express his teachings. To this reality, the Scriptures stand as a perpetual witness.

8. DO YOU BELIEVE THAT THERE ARE SEVEN SACRAMENTS?

§ YES

I think that this question attempts to ask more than is evident at first glance. What is intended is to find out what I really believe about the sacraments in general. Let me say that I do believe that there are seven sacraments, and not two or four, as some Protestants believe. I profess belief in the sacraments because the New Testament mentions all seven sacraments more or less openly. If you go through John, Paul, and the Acts, it is not difficult to find evidence of the institution of the seven sacraments. Tradition also teaches us that there are seven sacraments. Tradition is the teaching of the Church as handed down to us from the Apostles and the early Fathers of the Church.

I believe a sacrament to be an outward sign instituted by Christ to give grace. Thus a sacrament is not simply an arbitrary ceremony or a mere symbolic ritual. A sacrament is a gift of God, and more than merely signifying grace, it is the cause of its effect, that is, it is responsible for the increase of sanctifying and habitual grace within a soul. Belief in this automatic increase of grace has been criticized in the past, and some have said this gives a magical dimension to the sacraments. On the contrary. Although a person in mortal sin can be validly baptized, the effect of grace within him is in proportion to his willingness to receive that grace. The sacraments demand a proper disposition for their effective reception.

The very definition of a sacrament indicates that it is not an empty ritual, for a sacrament changes a person, introducing him, as in the case of baptism, to the life of the supernatural and removing him from the dominion of the devil. Because I appreciate the nature of the sacraments, I shudder to imagine what would happen if any of the sacraments were discontinued. As Catholics we depend on the sacraments for the continuation of a God-life within our souls. Each sacrament is a means of Christ acting in us and directing our destiny.

All the sacraments, then, are precious to me, especially when I realize that the efficacy of each sacrament cannot be impaired, no matter what the disposition of its minister. I receive Christ in the Eucharist even if the priest is in mortal sin. I do not agree with Zwingli that the sacraments are mere symbols of Christian belief, and I have perfect trust in God's providence and in the wisdom of the Church that Catholics will never be deprived of the sacraments.

✳ NO

I am reminded of someone who said that the Catholic Church is a religion of numbers. There are seven sacraments, three persons in one God, ten commandments, six precepts, four cardinal virtues, and so on. Religion is catalogued and reduced to stereotypes. I cannot limit the sacraments to a specific number any more than I can accept the definition of "sacrament" as mere ritual.

A sacrament is for me a sign of Christ's presence, and I like to think of the work of the famed Dutch theologian, E. Schillebeecks, O.P., on the nature of Christ as the prime sacrament. I think that today there are few theologians who would restrict the sacraments to seven, and most of them seem to glory in the extension of the term to more facets of human life.

Sacramental theology in the past limited itself to a mere explanation of matter and form, trying to determine how best to express the presence of Christ in symbol and in scholastic terminology. I remember witnessing an ordination to the priesthood and overhearing seminarians arguing about when exactly the sacrament of holy orders was conferred: Was it at the imposition of hands, or at some other high point in the ceremony? Sacramental theology emphasized rubrics, whereby minute details were legislated for the proper conferring of the sacrament. If any detail was omitted, then Christ would flee with his whole bag of grace.

Sacramental theology encouraged scrupulosity in the penitent. Did I confess all my mortal sins? Did I forget to tell the priest about the time that such and such happened? Did I sneeze during the consecration of the bread and thereby omit part of the response? And so on and so on, ad nauseam.

When the first light of suspicion was cast on the sacraments, quite a few people screamed heresy. Yet that magical invocation of the presence of Christ through ritualistic mumblings and anointings was dubious should have been obvious to any intelligent person. In its emphasis on the rubric of the sacrament, the Church has overlooked the disposition necessary for a worthy witness to Christ. Part of the disenchantment of many with the new liturgy stems from the traditional emphasis on excessive detail in worship.

I see anything that reminds me of God or of man's dignity as a sacrament. I can increase my own worth and that of the human race if I give of myself and my talents to ease the gnawing pain of a person in need. I don't have to speculate on how much grace I have received, nor do I yearn for a halo of saintliness for my activity. I simply see need and know that Christ is present in that need; he has taken flesh again, and he calls forth a response from me. Thus sign, efficacy, and Christ-origin are preserved, and my religion takes on more meaning and a wider scope.

I still believe the traditional concept of baptism and the other sacraments as grace-giving, but they become so as experiences for me, not mere ritual. I don't think of the sacraments in the abstract any more. I find Christ presents himself in more ways than seven, and this discovery enriches me.

9. DO YOU THINK TRADITION HAS BEEN OVEREMPHASIZED IN CATHOLICISM?

§   NO

Tradition, as everyone knows, is an important part of any organization. In our own government we lean heavily on tradition, and we know that most of our direction is achieved from a faithful adherence to it.

For Catholics, Tradition has been one of the twin sources of revelation. Tradition is the preachings of the Church. It is the handing down, *tradere*, by the Church of the revelation of Christ and the Holy Spirit to the Apostles. Many people make the mistake of thinking that Tradition is simply an adulation of past forms. But Tradition is not confined to the past; it is the perpetual preservation and faithful implementation of Christ's teaching. Tradition demands life, or else it becomes pure history. Through Tradition the Church is constantly aware of her mission to defend the teachings of God.

The theory of Tradition is that the Church has received the deposit of faith, and that it must always be aware of the reality of this treasure, seeking to defend it at all times and guaranteeing that no arbitrary changes will be made. Isn't this what Pope Paul stated? He sees himself as the guardian of our sacred Tradition, and let it be known that when it comes to matters of doctrine and faith, he is unyielding.

The infamous Dutch catechism is under heavy fire from orthodox theologians because it allows a weak explanation of our traditional beliefs and, in so doing, opens up the possibility of misinterpretations of the deposit of faith.

Tradition is a living reality, and through it the Church constantly shows its awareness of its vocation as defender of the faith. Catholics thus place great emphasis on Tradition, since Tradition is living, constant, and vital.

Tradition is, then, the teaching of the Church, or what is known as the magisterium. The Church has received the Bible as the registry of God's revelation. It interprets the Scriptures and determines which writings are divinely revealed. Although the Church uses the Scriptures, it maintains that in Tradition alone is God's revelation integrally placed. Thus the Church does not depend on the Scriptures alone to justify its teachings, since it is the teaching instrument founded by Christ himself. The vocation of the Church is to transmit the divine revelation through its teaching.

Some say that the Church neglects the Bible and puts greater emphasis on the concept of Tradition. Actually, God's revelation has been given to us through two sources, the inspired writings of the Scriptures and the inspired teachings of the Church. Because the Scriptures are not an organized credo or a set of dogmatic principles, it is the obligation of the Church to make the necessary interpretations so that what is found in the Bible can be faithfully adhered to.

The Bible and Tradition go hand in hand, but it is Tradition that guards the precious deposit of faith. It is the obligation of each generation to pass on the gift of faith to its children. It is here that Tradition makes its greatest contribution.

❇ YES

Tradition is understood as the living teaching of the Church. But Tradition has been overemphasized to the point that the Bible has been regarded as inconsequential. We have substituted organized religion and ritual for revelation. Tradition has been misused; one evidence of this is the need of the Church to declare the Pope infallible. If it were certain that God's word is found in Scripture, then we would have no need to arm the defender of that doctrine, which is precisely what the doctrine of infallibility does.

Tradition is supposed to be something living, something vital, but in the past it has been restrictive and containing. Tradition should not imply the static and the hoary, but should lead to deeper and clearer insights into the revealed word of God. There should be a closer relationship between Scripture and Tradition, a sense of communication between the two. And this we have not seen in the history of the Church. Vatican II stated that both Scripture and Tradition flow from the same wellspring and merge into a unity, tending toward the same goal, which is to help bring about a better understanding of God by man.

Vatican II restored the proper balance between Tradition, the teaching of the Church, and Scripture, by showing that Tradition should be a living explanation of the divine writings and not merely an iron-clad array of cold, static dogmas. Tradition should interpret the teachings of God, and in this sense Tradition serves the divine word. It draws from the Gospels everything that it presents as divinely revealed.

What we need now is a return to the true spirit of Scripture, especially of the Gospels. We have to replace legalism with evangelism, that is, canon law and abstract theology must bow before the will of God as found in the Gospel. What we have seen happen in the Church is a reduction of Tradition to mere factual knowledge and technical skill. How well a dogma was phrased became more important than how credible was its content.

Tradition should express art, language, political realities, a way of life, and a community of experience. What we have witnessed is a Tradition that became a depository for pet theories in theology. Tradition invests the Church with a sense of dignity, but Tradition should also be a source of credibility. If the deposit of faith becomes caked with anachronistic forms, then Tradition has failed. Tradition in fact has betrayed its role.

In the Church today there are those who believe that traditionalism in synonymous with Tradition. But traditionalism is very often reactionism, pure and simple. We have to separate Tradition from doctrine and discipline, for these latter cannot claim the direct authority of God revealing himself. True Tradition is the abiding presence of God in history, and the Church must see its role as preserving this presence and making it ever more real and credible.

I like to look upon Tradition as teaching the sacred writings through example. Far from being a block to a rewarding God-relationship, Tradition should be a spur, an inspiration, and must ever be faithful to its role of teaching through example.

10. DO YOU STILL ABSTAIN
     FROM MEAT ON FRIDAYS?

§   YES

I think most people forget that when the Church changed the law about eating meat on Friday, it made abstinence optional. The same motivation for abstinence exists, namely, mortification. The fact that so few people today still follow this ancient and revered tradition now that it is an optional exercise proves that they were simply obeying out of fear.

Abstinence and mortification have always been considered

salutary exercises throughout the history of religion. Even the pagans mortified themselves to discipline the body. Athletes today realize that optimum bodily control can be attained only through specific discipline. The laws of fast and abstinence were modified because the pressures of the times made them too burdensome for most Catholics.

It was never the intention of the Church to imply that meat and other foods are evil in themselves. Rather, the law had as its goal the developing of will power, the practice of temperance and moderation. The law also tried to nudge people into doing penance for their sins. In the Old Testament we read of people offering to God the first fruits of the harvest and symbolizing their dependence on God through sacrifice and penance. I abstain from meat on Friday not because I have to, but because I want to deny myself, to offer sacrifice for my sins, and also because I thereby perform an act of homage to the Creator. I acknowledge that God is the source of all my blessings and that he gives and takes away.

I find more meaning in mortification now that I am not obligated to do penance, but I regret that the Church has acquiesced in the weakness of modern man by abolishing fasting and abstinence. I think that a mistake was made because more and more people are doing less and less penance. At Fatima, Our Lady stressed the notion of penance, and at Lourdes she cried out that penance was a necessary factor in any relationship with God. The world today is going through such agonizing times because man refuses to accept the need for pain and suffering in his own life. He is unwilling to accept pain for the love of God and the salvation of souls. Few today have the maturity to take the path of penance and mortification on their own. And it seems to me that God is punishing us because man refuses to recognize the power and greatness of his Creator.

❋ NO

I don't abstain on Friday, and, to be honest, I ate meat on Friday even when the Church said it was a mortal sin. I always considered that law rather infantile, and so, in good conscience,

I gave my attention to more important considerations. I don't think it is the role of the Church to make up menus or plan a person's life in detail. I am not against penance and mortification, but I discipline myself through realistic involvement in my fellow man's problems.

I am happy to see that the ritualistic approach to salvation is fast disappearing. Some Catholics label its disappearance a cause of current disaster. These fish-on-Friday Catholics don't know where to turn for masochistic thrills, and they spend their time carping and lampooning the trend toward renewal in the Church. I have always considered Lent and Advent gloomy times of the year. The ashes, the doleful music, the somber purple in the churches never lifted up my soul to the Lord. When Easter came finally, I remember as a kid I breathed a sigh of relief that all the lamenting and bone rattling were over.

Religion is supposed to be something joyful. If we have discovered God, we should at least be happy about it. "Gospel" means "good news," and religion should concern itself with the Gospel. Religion means that God has not rejected man, but is with him always. Religion should be a joyful message from God to man. The stress today is on responsibility, rewarding experiences, and renewed motivation.

Penance and mortification must be decided by the individual; his own need to transform pain and suffering into an energizing force in the world should be his only guide. I will respect a person who abstains from meat on Friday because he is trying thereby to strengthen his God-relationship. But because pain and suffering are so personal and so deep, I cannot accept the fact that any organized religion has the right to impose them on a person.

V

SIN

FROM THE BEGINNING of time, fear has been a part of man. Early man was afraid of thunder, of fire, of wild beasts. But most of all he seems to have been afraid of himself. He was always fearful that his actions might offend his deities.

The human race has grown up somewhat. We are no longer unduly fearful of thunder, fire, or wild beasts. We have conquered nature. But we have not conquered ourselves. We still fear—in an almost manic way—that we will commit sin.

What is this mysterious thing we fear? The Church teaches us what sin is: a violation of the laws of God. The Church, after having defined and set down the laws of God, catalogued the various violations that could be committed against these laws. As a universal Church, it is able to make these categories apply to all peoples.

The Church has a hierarchy of values. The most important thing is not simply to avoid sin, but to love God and neighbor. But the Church, in its wisdom, realizes that love is a pretty tenuous ideal, that it cannot be achieved without a strict enforcement of laws. Thus the emphasis on conformity to the laws of the Church and the tirades against sin.

Because of this, our lives as Catholics are filled with fear—fear of breaking the rules—and with guilt—guilt for having done wrong. We all do wrong. Who has not heard that "even the just man sins seven times daily"?

Some people feel this emphasis on sin is unhealthy, that it is opposed to the basic tenets of modern psychology, that it is unnatural, unreal. Is sin really the wicked giant blocking the doorway to heaven? they ask. Is it a sword hanging over our heads, just waiting for the chance to catch us off guard? Is the Church itself sinning by making us neurotics, fearful of our own shadow? Shouldn't love be a positive force, not merely the result of the fear of doing evil?

We think that it is a healthy step to rethink our attitudes toward sin as set forth in the following questions.

1. IS THERE SUCH A THING AS ORIGINAL SIN?

§ YES

Original sin is a reality because the Church teaches us it is so. The Church cannot err in questions of faith and morals.

Original sin is seen in man's fallen nature. It has darkened man's intellect and crippled his will.

Even though original sin is a doctrine of the Church, it is common sense too. The evidence of sin and evil is everywhere. Cardinal Newman once said, "If there be a God, since there is a God, the human race is implicated in some terrible aboriginal calamity. It is out of joint with the purposes of its Creator. This is a fact, a fact as true as the fact of man's existence."

Original sin affects me personally. I'm not as good as I want to be. I don't do the job I should do. I know that my baptism washed away original sin. I don't know why I am one of those chosen by God to have received this great blessing, but I thank him for his mercy.

Through the Church I know what must be done to attain eternal salvation. Without the Church I would flounder. I know that I have God's help and the Church's protection. Knowing this makes life easier and more hopeful.

The world is evil, and man, although he was created for God, seems to seek that evil as the easy way out. The Church alone can show me the way out of this valley of tears. Without the Church I would be left to my own evil nature.

✳ NO

The doctrine of original sin presents many problems. The doctrine as it stands represents a naïve man-God relationship. The biblical source cited as supporting this doctrine is a myth, according to modern exegetical scholarship.

In its doctrine of original sin, just what is the Church trying to say? Is sin, purportedly a personal act, actually collective? Are unbaptized children inheritors of some type of guilt, some type of shame? Did Christ save all men by his death, or are we still under the domination of this original sin?

In our advanced scientific civilization the doctrine of original sin cannot stand. It makes a person insecure, anxious, and guilt-ridden; it makes him feel less a human being. Isn't it possible for people to know, love, and serve God without first having to be clubbed into submission?

Of course there is evil in the world. Every one of us often fails in what we want to do. But this lack of perfection is not something unnatural. It is the Church, after all, that claims that man is God-like naturally, and animal-like only unnaturally through sin. We must work to improve ourselves, there is no doubt of that. We cannot be satisfied with our present condition. But we need not condemn ourselves to a guilty and fearful existence under the illusion that we are hopeless sinners.

If more people questioned this doctrine, then perhaps the Church would give us a better understanding of original sin and its effects. Perhaps the Church will let us hold our heads high, confident in the realization that although we have a lot of improving to do, we are constantly evolving closer to our goal, God, who is goodness himself.

2. IS MAN REALLY A SINNER?

§ YES

It is important always to keep in mind how man started out. In the beginning we were no better than savages. As the centuries passed, we improved primarily because of the influence of religion. The Jews with the help of the Hebrew God, Yahweh, moved mankind forward. Christians, with the benefit of the full revelation of Christ, have made great progress. Christ gave us all the help we need to live a perfect and holy life. Of course, we don't do as well as we should, but this is further proof that we are basically sinners.

If we had not received the revelation of God, we would be totally degenerate, because it is our nature to avoid doing the best we can.

What need do we have of God, if we are not basically sinners? If we were not wrongdoers, we would not be dependent on him, as we would always avoid evil.

Some people who claim not to believe in God do good work, of course, but how long can that last? Also, I know that it is only God's influence on them that allows them to do good, even if they don't accept this fact. Remember what Christ said: "Without me you can do nothing."

✴ NO

To say that we are naturally sinners is an insult to any intelligent man. To be a sinner means to be a person who is dishonest with himself, a person who is deliberately fooling himself about reality. I reject the idea that without external help all men would be sinful.

God made all men. Civilization has greatly improved, and the credit for this belongs to man, to his ingenuity and creativity. Man is God's greatest masterpiece, and man is free with the freedom of the children of God. To say that he is self-destructive and a negative force in the world is untrue.

Man, of course, can be cruel, dishonest, insincere. Writers in particular like to make capital on this point. For example the book *Lord of the Flies* can easily be seen as a parable on man's disposition to evil. But while I appreciated the book's significance I cannot accept it as a total view of man. Such a reversion to savagery as described in the book is possible but I'm convinced that man has an even greater potential in the opposite direction. It is this direction toward good that we must look to if we are to find hope for a truly human man.

Man's pride in himself is a relatively recent phenomenon, and this trend was started by people who have rejected the Church's negative approach toward man. Now it is up to the Church to admit its own frailty and accept this happy development. If the Church continues to hold onto its destructive belief,

then it will be left behind in the dust caused by the progress that
real men are making.

3. IS THERE SUCH A THING AS SIN?

§ YES

How can one look at the many horrible things taking place
in the world today—how can one look at all these evil things and
ask whether sin is being committed? The Church is quite clear
about what sin is, and about the fact that sin is the main cause of
trouble in the world. This is the difference between this and the
next world: in heaven we will be free from sin.

My whole spiritual life is based on the premise that there is
such a thing as sin and that we must do our utmost to avoid this
specter. The manuals on spiritual life, the books on asceticism,
offer plans that can take us step by step away from sin and toward
perfection. If there were no sin in us, then we would be perfect
already, and it is quite obvious that we are not. All of us have a
long way to go and the sooner we realize it, the sooner the world
will be on its way to perfection.

❋ NO

There is no such thing as sin that is the root of all our problems. Man is not perfect, and he can improve himself, but I cannot accept the basic assumption that man is born evil and must
spend most of his time avoiding sin. Christ redeemed us. We can
be insincere, we can fail to do what is right, we can sin, but let's
not make sin the rockbed of our existence. This world is filled
with goodness, and it is with goodness that we start on our
Christian journey.

Who is it that stresses sin so much? Isn't it the Church?
Doesn't the Church make us fearful and negative in our approach
to life? After all, if you took away the idea of sin, then there
would be no need for laws. The Church as an institution thrives

on laws and regulations. A catalogue of wrongs is an essential part of an institution such as the Church. Creative and positive thinking—the results of freedom from the law and from fear of sin—is hard to catalogue and regulate. If we want this freedom we must get it ourselves.

4. IS THERE AN OBJECTIVE MORALITY?

§ YES

Anyone who believes in God, and believes that God is one, good, and true, must realize that there can be only one truth. Morality is man's relationship to truth. There can be only one morality. If there were no one, true, and objective morality, anarchy would be supreme. Man would do anything he wanted to other men. There could be no law, there could be no order. The radicals who claim to want freedom do not realize what untrammeled freedom will lead to.

Fortunately the Church is courageously holding on to the truth and the value of an objective morality. As the official voice of God, it can never lose sight of its role in setting moral standards. In a sense, the Church is the loving parent who censures any child who begins to stray from the way of truth and justice and morality. It is a narrow way, and the Church often feels hard put to keep her children on it. There have been many examples of the Church's parental concern. At the beginning of the twentieth century the Church condemned what it called the Modernist heresy. Later, it condemned the heresy of our day, communism. Without the Church's courageous and critical judgment of communism, this atheistic philosophy would be even more powerful than it is.

The Church is also careful about the way in which the faithful view morality. It is constantly advising us to heed its word on matters of morals. The Church is infallible on such matters, and it has been teaching the same morality for many centuries. We can't go wrong by obeying the Church.

Those who want to create a new morality speak of the new sexual, intellectual, and religious freedoms. But we must always remember that in matters of religion, like everything else, there is not much new under the sun. God is the light. He is the truth, and he is eternal. The truth never changes, and neither does morality. It is the same for everybody in all ages.

❋ NO

There is no objective morality. Truth is in the person, and every person is different. Morality is in the person, and so every person must form his own morality.

I'm so tired of hearing people talking about morality as the will of God. Who can say for sure what God wants us to do? Who claims to speak for the God who is not present to every man? The Church does, but before we accept it as the final authority, we should look to see if it practices what it preaches. We can even ask: It is possible to practice what the Church preaches? I remember a young Jew complaining that the religious leaders of his time have multiplied the laws and so burdened the people that they can only stagger under the load.

The moral system of the Church is supposed to apply to every person on earth. Look what happened when the missionaries carried this universal morality to a cultured and civilized people of the Far East. Today the Chinese are under the dominion of a system diametrically opposed to Catholic morality. Much of the blame for this is due to the unyielding view the missionaries took toward the customs of the people and the refusal of the Church to let them worship in their own language. In Africa the missionaries cover the breasts of the native women in order to save their purity (whose purity?). In Japan the missionaries continued to use black vestments at Masses for the dead, even though black in Japan is the color of rejoicing. How immoral the Church has been in its attempts to force its own ideas and customs on other cultured peoples!

Every person must be free to find himself and develop his own morality. This will not lead to anarchy but will develop creative, responsible people, not puppets led by the moral strings of the Catholic Church.

5. ARE LAWS THE SOLUTION TO AVOIDING SIN?

§ YES

Our first responsibility as a Christian is to love God. Then we must love our neighbor. Love is our vocation. But history has taught us that love without laws is bound to fail. Laws are our only hope for salvation. Without them we would not know how to love. I don't think that the Church for all the lip service it has given to the statement of St. Augustine, has ever really believed that you can love and then do what you will. That's a great goal, but someone has to be practical enough to provide a means to reach that goal. Only saints are totally driven by love. The rest of us must constantly strive toward this perfection but must always lean on the helpful, supporting arm of Church law.

We can love only if there is true peace, and peace means the harmony of nature, the right order of nature. Order can only come about through a strict observance of law. Our laws, then, must take care of the many practical issues that we run into every day of our lives. That's why it is difficult to accept the Church's capitulation to some of the "new" theologians and its relaxation of some of its laws. For example, the laws on penance and mortification, such as abstaining from meat on Friday and fasting during Lent have helped me greatly during my weaker moments. Now, even though laws concerning mortification have been taken off the books, I will always keep them in mind so that I can continue to avoid sin as much as possible. But I fear for my children and my grandchildren. Who will guide them? Without the Church and her laws, I cannot see much hope for them and their faith. I only hope that the Church has not modernized itself too much.

✳ NO

Christ came to free us from laws. He set up no formal regulations during his lifetime. He did not follow the law of the
leaders of his religion. He was a rebel—a positive rebel. That is all
he asks of us. He told us that we would always run into opposition
when we practiced his ideas, but it is sad when the institution
opposing us is the very Church that he founded.

Laws restrict, stifle, and suffocate. Laws are for children.
Grown men should not be led by the nose. Creativity is the search
for the constant newness of God and of other men. Creativity is
our response to God's love for us. Creativity is refusal to conform
to the unreal structures into which others want to fit us. Creativity
is love, and love is limitless. We might still fail, we will still make
mistakes, but we will grow, we will advance in wisdom, age, and
grace before God and man.

6. WILL GOD PUNISH US FOR OUR SINS?

§ YES

This is the ultimate question when one starts questioning the
existence of sin. If we start wondering whether there is sin, and
whether sin or morality can be objective, then we must come down
to the question: Does sin have any final effect on our lives? The
Church teaches us that on the final day we will be judged for our
sins, and that if we are found to be sinful we will be punished
forever in hell. I believe this. If we are not to be punished for our
sins, then why not just go out and sin?

If citizens were not punished for their crimes against society,
do you think that they would obey laws? Of course not. Murders,
robberies, rapes, kidnappings, and other horrible crimes would be
the order of the day.

It's the same way in the spiritual realm. If we did not think
that we would be punished for the sins we commit, we would be

free to do anything we wished. We could disobey the laws of the Church, we could flout the Ten Commandments, we could ignore God. And then how could God judge us? Why should we then be rewarded with heaven? Fear of the Lord is a good thing, and we should all fear his punishment, for it will surely come on the last day if we are found lacking.

※ NO

I also agree that this is the ultimate question. It determines our attitude toward our whole life. It is ridiculous to think that on the last day, whenever that is, we will be judged on the basis of what sins we have avoided. You may say that you will really be judged on how much love you have for God and neighbor, but it all comes down to what sins you've not committed. Imagine going to heaven because you never missed Mass on Sunday, or because you never ate meat on Friday. Or, even worse, imagine going to hell because you did miss Mass on Sunday.

Our whole Catholic life is based on fear. See how we fear one another and our world! We can't try anything new, we can't be creative, because it might be against the laws of the Church, and if we break those laws, we will be punished. We can't think on our own, because the only things we are supposed to think about are found in the Bible and in the Tradition of the Church, and if we don't follow them, we will be punished. The Christian life of the Western world is based on reward/punishment: Do this and you shall have life. Do that and you shall be doomed forever. That's no way to live. We've got to give ourselves credit for honesty and for creativeness. We've got to "do our thing," because ours is the only thing we can do.

A young actor on a television talk show said that he doesn't have time to worry about the morals of other people. He said that he was only an individual, and he could only know how he felt about his own moral life. Although some people reacted against him, I think that he spoke very well, and I don't think he was being selfish. He didn't say that he was unconcerned about the welfare of other people, but that he had to find out who he was himself before he could understand others. I remember hearing a young Jew saying something similar: Before you try to take the splinter out of someone else's eye, look to the beam in your own eye.

We can't live our lives in fear of how other people—or even God—will judge us. Christ said: "Seek first the kingdom of God, and the kingdom of God is within you." We must first be true to ourselves, and we cannot do this if we are living in fear. God will not punish us for our sins. But he will reward us for our creative and personal response to his love.

7. IS MORTIFICATION AN ESSENTIAL PART OF CHRISTIAN LIFE?

§ YES

Not only is mortification an important part of Christian life, but it is part of most religions of the world. One of the essential Buddhist methods of reaching perfection is to destroy all desires. Christians don't attempt to go that far. We want to deprive the flesh so that the spirit may be raised up to God. We want to vitiate all earthly desires so that we desire God with our whole being. This is what heaven will be: a concern for nothing but the presence of God.

We reach this state more quickly through mortification. We must suffer either on this earth or in the afterlife of hell or purgatory. Suffering on this earth is far preferable. The very act of mortification is a sign of our goal: we despise earthly goods because they will be replaced by heavenly reward. Christ himself told us: "Seek first the kingdom of heaven, and all else will be given to you besides." By mortifying ourselves, we place ourselves in opposition to this world so that we may better approach God's kingdom.

Most sins are caused by evil desires. Because it is often difficult to detect good from evil, it is best to curb all our appetites so that we don't fall into any traps. Thus it is good practice to give up some small thing, such as a tempting snack, so that we might be better prepared to face the bigger temptations that await us constantly.

I know people who don't mortify themselves. They have no system to their lives, no direction. They do what they want to do, and they satisfy their every whim. What will happen to them will be the satiation of all desire: gross despair. Look at what many of the saints experienced before they were converted. St. Augustine regretted his wild, libertine younger days. He continually felt guilt over his will-less and wanton theft of apples. Many of his actions, of course, were not as horrible as he made them out to be, but they are examples of actions that proper mortification would have prevented.

I'm not against joy and laughter. These have their place in life. After all, a sad saint is a sorry saint. But we must remember that we are always bent toward the earth, and away from God. If we want to be true sons of God and brothers of Christ, we must constantly attempt to rise above our flesh by mortifying it. Without sincere and constant mortification, we can hardly live in union with the spirit of Christ given to us in baptism.

❋ NO

When I hear all this talk about mortification, I am reminded of a little child who has been told that he can't have any candy before supper. To get even with the world, the child refuses to eat his supper, even though he would enjoy it. Or the child who throws his erector set away when he is told to stop breaking it, meaning, "If I can't abuse it, I won't even use it!"

Christ came to earth to put our priorities straight. The Jews had begun to seek truth and beauty where they can never be found: in dominion over others, in pride of race over all other races, in a rigid system of overbearing regulations. Christ showed them where God really is: in the lilies of the field, in the widow who was generous even to her last cent, in the children who came to him. He told the Jews: Don't go ruining what is in the world by using it the wrong way; find out what is beautiful in the world. But what have our religious leaders done throughout history? They have tried to inscribe in our hearts the saying: "If you can't abuse it, don't even use it!"

We have been created in God's image, and so we must act

like God. We must *create* with all the talents that we have. Nothing—nothing whatsoever—must keep us from this goal. A famous song and comedy writer has a humorous yet very effective motto: "Self-Indulgence Pays." I think Christianity should take a deeper look at this more-than-playful slogan.

The main reason that mortification is a short-sighted and impotent approach to Christian living is that it very rarely takes the present into account. The typical approach to mortification is: "If I sacrifice in this small way now, I will be able to avoid falling into temptation ten years from now." This is a very mathematical approach to a life style that should be formed by the same sense of mission that motivated Christ. Time is constructed in such a way that the future can be confronted some time in the future. The present is what is important now. Whenever I meet one of these future-oriented mortifiers, I am tempted to walk up to him and suddenly say: "I am the Great Talent Collector. What have you got for me?" I wonder what he would say.

8. IS THE NATURAL LAW MAN-MADE?

§   NO

It's important to remember that man is merely one segment in the hierarchy of creation. Only when we see the many other levels of existence—mineral, vegetable, and animal life, angelic life, and God—can we see ourselves in perspective. All these forms of life have a law that governs their existence. Thus, a rock can't propel itself; a bird can't speak intelligently; a man can't fly. Now man is part animal, so he is bound by the same physical laws that bind the animals. But man is also part spirit and thus is governed by a special type of moral law, which we call natural law. All men feel the effects of this important and necessary code that speaks to man through his conscience. Thus all men feel that it is evil to kill or to steal another person's property. To say, then, that the natural law is man-made is to say that a particular person or culture has set up an arbitrary system of rules and forced it on all men. Such a statement contradicts all the evidence of history.

Even the most primitive men responded to the haunting and never-ceasing call of their consciences. Even though man's conscience has been refined through the ages as he improved his civilization, still this inner champion of a moral code—natural law—has always been heard.

But we must go deeper than that. Some people do claim that the natural law is actually not natural, but man-made. A statement like that tends to destroy all respect for God's power over his created universe. Natural law stems from God's dominion over all his creation. If he doesn't have universal control, how can he be truly God, the all-powerful being? If his laws are not the same everywhere, then how can he be truth? If people are free to do whatever they please, then where is goodness? Where is God? I believe God is truth and goodness, so these thoughts are not even problems for me. But how can anyone who claims to believe in God doubt the universal rule of God? If we believe in God, we've got to believe in certain corollaries. The Church has always taught the existence of natural law. We've got to believe it if we want to remain Catholics. To say that the natural law is man-made is to say that God himself is man-made.

❋ YES

Natural law has been pushed on us by people who are fearful of anarchy and division. Remember that this natural law has had to be written down for us many times. It seems that someone is afraid that we will forget it. I sincerely believe that by pushing natural law so hard we have made it completely unnatural. We have dressed it in a fancy coat and tie when it feels much more comfortable in a simple birthday suit. And where has this brought us? We are bound by laws we don't understand. We repeat by rote the Ten Commandments and claim that this is our expression of the natural law and the sum of our natural existence. We pass judgment on any who don't follow these "preordained" precepts.

Our concept of natural law is concerned too much with law and not enough with nature. And our moral law is altogether arbitrary. It's simple to come up with specialized, almost private, interpretations of what our nature and our natural law are. The natural law against killing is quite explicit. Yet who are the heroes of any society throughout history? Aren't they the soldiers, the people who kill as part of the jobs? Despite the natural law, war has never been considered illegal. A man might be punished severely for stealing some insignificant item, but this same man is a hero if he is lucky enough to return from a violent battle. And what other natural laws are broken in war, during which, as in love, all is fair? So who interprets this natural law? Is it not man? And how poor a job he does of it!

If man is honest with himself and the people around him, the world will be in good shape naturally. A perfectly free man is a perfectly natural man. If we are going to talk about man and his destiny we need to talk less of natural law and more of natural trust.

9. AREN'T "OCCASIONS OF SIN" FIGMENTS OF A SUPERSTITIOUS IMAGINATION?

§   NO

An occasion of sin is any situation, person, or thing that can lead me into foresaking God and doing evil. Who can deny that such occasions exist? Many people complacently smirk at any reference to the battle between good and evil, between God and the devil. But this battle does exist, and it has grown even fiercer in our own day. Immorality, especially immorality of the body, is rampant, and everyone knows that temptations of the flesh are Satan's chief method of attack. Religion today is hard put to defend itself against the inroads of atheism and antireligious forces. Consciously or not, many people in the entertainment business are counted among the devil's brigade because of the evil influence they have upon society. Much of this occurs because the occasions of sin are not recognized.

The battle between good and evil is very real. But it is not a pitched, open fight. The devil is too wily for that. He knows that he can't win the ultimate battle, so he tries his best to trick and beguile people onto his side. The fight is more like guerrilla warfare—insidious, sudden, deadly. Books, movies, pictures, unrestrained and frivolous talk—all these are examples of traps set for the unsuspecting individual. It is the job of every Catholic to avoid such moral pitfalls by being constantly on the alert. Any intelligent soldier would take every precaution to ensure his safe journey through a dark jungle in Vietnam. The enemy might not be visible, but he is certainly there. We are soldiers of Christ, and we must believe, for the very safety of our souls, that Satan is waiting in ambush.

We don't live in a vacuum, though. Sometimes we will be directly confronted with an occasion of sin. Then we can do nothing but rely on the grace of God to strengthen us throughout the struggle. If we have taken the proper precautions, God's grace will be sufficient for us. But we must do our best to avoid these confrontations. We must have a healthy fear of the devil and his wiles.

The best way to aid Satan in his struggle to overcome goodness is to pretend that he doesn't exist. People who spoof Satan's existence are his easiest prey. The sad part is that most often they don't even realize that they are under his thumb. Certain modern philosophers and atheistic scientists claim to be free from the myths of religion. But rather, they are linked to the invisible but ever-growing chain with which Satan is trying to enslave the world. We can turn back this evil tide by avoiding and exposing the many occasions of sin that are lurking to trap us.

❄ *YES*

That people of past centuries could live by a belief in occasions of sin is understandable. But man has become more and more the master of his destiny, and he has less reason to put up with such ideas. We must reject such myths for what they are. Does the devil exist? Does the Good Fairy exist? In my mind both questions are the same. The Good Fairy is a folk-tale creation. And that's all. Yet students of Christianity are told to see Satan as a very real factor in the history of the real world. And that's too much.

Does evil exist? That's another question. I've never seen good or evil. But I have seen good people and bad people. That is where we must look for qualities of goodness and badness: in people. Each one of us has experienced the evil tendencies in ourselves. One philosopher describes it this way: A person is driving along a mountain road thinking about the danger of driving off the cliff. Suddenly he feels an urge to go over the edge. Later on, he fearfully wonders why such a self-destructive desire should be so powerful in him. Thus this man is confronted with the complexity of his life. He is a powerhouse of constructive and destructive energies, of "good" and "evil" tendencies. To ascribe such feelings to a supernatural influence is totally unreal and mythical. Even the Church agrees that it is poor practice to find supernatural reasons for an event when natural reasons will supply the answer.

With such an attitude in mind, I cannot categorize certain situations or things as occasions of sin. An art film that depicts nudity might be an erotic experience for an immature person and a total bore for a married couple. A discussion that criticizes the politics of government or Church might offend the sensibilities of the charitable Christian, but for an action-oriented person such criticism might offer constructive ideas. There is good and evil, but it is not just floating around; it is in ourselves. To recognize good and evil, we must be willing to express our complex selves. Fear of evil, fear of one's self, is the surest and quickest road to self-destruction. We can use anything for good if we know ourselves and have confronted our own complex attitudes toward life.

10. IS IT A GOOD THING FOR RELIGION TO MAKE PEOPLE FEEL GUILTY?

§ YES

Christianity is a joyful religion. But this joy must always be tempered by the realization that we are sinners and in need of redemption. Christ saved all men once and for all; this is the objective redemption. But each one of us must be redeemed individually, and this is what is called the subjective redemption. It is in this second area that guilt is helpful. Guilt makes a person aware of his constant sinfulness and thus helps him to know himself better. In this way he is more easily able to keep on the straight and narrow path that Christ laid out for us.

Fear of the Lord is a healthy attitude, and Christianity recognizes this truth. If we can maintain a proper sense of guilt over our failings we will be less likely to sin than if we rely completely on idealistic hope and joy. These have their place, of course, but they must be kept there. The Church strongly urges all its members to repeat the Act of Contrition at least every day. A daily examination of conscience is also a proper aid to gaining a deeper understanding of one's sinfulness. Finally, the sacrament of penance should be received often, so that we may have our sins washed away and be better able to avoid sin in the future. Thus the Church properly emphasizes the role of sin in our lives, and by making us feel guilt it helps bring us closer to the sinless Lord who became man for us.

The Catholic Church is a church not only for its members, but for the whole world. Christ's last command was that his Church spread the Gospel everywhere. The Church best performs this mission by showing the world for what it is. In the light of the Church's holiness, the world looks very sinful indeed. This is what the Church wants to do: when the world experiences guilt in the presence of the Church, it will be more likely to come to grips with the reality that is Christ. Thus the Church uses guilt as a catalyst to bring people into her holy fold.

The very basis of Christianity rests on the fact that we have been saved from sin. Our religious life should be a constant reaction against sin and a constant motion toward God. God has given us reason enough to love him. In turn, we must build up in ourselves a real revulsion against sin. We can do this by feeling an honest guilt over our own sinfulness, which we see more than enough of every day.

✳ *NO*

Ideal religion doesn't use guilt to enslave people. Religion as it has been practiced throughout history has made a great deal of guilt, but today people are beginning to reject such a negative approach to the most important aspect of a man's life—his relationship to God. An ideal religion should challenge men, should urge them to reach their utmost potential. Guilt is a suppressant and does nothing to uplift man. Organized religion has done much to encourage guilty feelings. It has sought to reinforce its own reason for existence by preying on people's fears and guilts and then offering a way to eradicate them.

What is the main concern of the typical Catholic today? Is it not his membership in the Church? Actions are performed or not performed on the basis of how such actions will affect his membership. I use the pedestrian term "membership" to designate union with the Church, for very few Catholics are taught to consider their religion anything else but a connection with an organization that has rules and regulations. Look what happened when Jacqueline Kennedy married Aristotle Onassis, a divorced man. The big question was: Is she still a member of the Church, or has she been excommunicated? The almost universal reaction of Catholics throughout the country was a revulsion against her flouting of the Church's divorce law. Very few seemed concerned with the fact that Mrs. Onassis might truly love Mr. Onassis. But in organized Catholicism, such ideas seem secondary.

Catholics have been trained to avoid action and involvement, for these might lead to errors that will cause guilt. Guilt becomes the overriding factor in a Catholic's life. Not love, not mission, not action.

What should religion demand of a person? What is the religious man's attitude toward life? Any intelligent person will recognize that man makes a lot of mistakes. He has made them in the past and he will continue to make them. But mistakes are made to be corrected, not mourned. A man's attitude toward failure will determine his level of success. The truly religious person is one who sees opportunity in the life he is living, even in the face of constant failure and error. The guilty person has no time to consider new paths because he is constantly wondering whether he should have taken some of the old ones. The creative person—the man who is most like God who is *the* Creator—is willing to make many mistakes to ensure a few successes. Sin? Sin is in the vocabulary of the guilty person only. The man who refuses to be snared by the spider web of guilt does not recognize the word. If sin is anything at all, it is an attitude, not an action. The creative man is confident that his attitude is sincere and practical. That is enough for him to act on.

Such an approach will not lead to utopia. It will not dissolve the complex and difficult problems that face our world today. But it will make the possibility of success much more real. And it will bring the reality of God much closer to all. For guilt can only snuff out hope and creativity. True religion can be guided by love alone, never by negative and destructive guilt.

VI
LIFE
HEREAFTER

SINCE CHILDHOOD you have probably sought the good things of life. At the same time, you have kept an eye on eternity lest death come and catch you like a thief in the night. Many people die suddenly, their lives brutally cut down. They are pictured as having one hand in the till when they are suddenly caught by death and asked to render an account of their stewardship.

Have you ever really examined the belief in a life hereafter? Do you think that death is the end of it all, or that another existence awaits us beyond the grave?

Almost assuredly, your entire life is conditioned by belief in life after death. The Church keeps you in line with the constant threat of eternal damnation. Are you satisfied to have a relationship with God that is built on fear and guilt? Do you honestly believe that there is room for love and genuine charity in such a relationship? Some would argue that St. John tells us that perfect love casts out fear and that the New Covenant is supposed to be one of love.

You have been told that hell is a place of eternal pain and punishment. But have you ever thought about hell? Is the conception of hell consonant with a God of love? Would God punish a person for human frailty? Some believe that the law of forgiveness Christ taught also applies to God the Father.

The concept of hell is supposedly built on the need for justice. You are told that no one is sent to hell by God, but that man himself is responsible for his own damnation because he has free will. The parable of Dives and Lazarus has often been used to justify eternal punishment. A person has to accept the responsibility of his choice, but how many people actually choose pain and eternal damnation over God? How many people actually know what God is? Don't you have to know both sides to make an intelligent choice? Some say, however, that ignorance is no excuse, and they condemn thousands to hell. How about you? What do you think? What are your ideas about eternal life?

1. IS LIFE HEREAFTER PIE IN THE SKY?

§ NO

To so characterize a basic belief of Christians is scandalous and irreverent. The concept of life hereafter is solidly based on the Scriptures and in the Tradition of the Church.

Catholics believe that death is not the end of everything. We believe in life after death. It is toward this belief that we direct our entire energy here on earth, so that our heaven will be crowned with glory. We believe that the soul is immortal, that it will never die. This is reasonable, since the soul is spiritual and not made up of material parts that can disintegrate.

We are not searching for some happy hunting ground. We are not escaping from life here on earth. We try to make the best use of our limited, imperfect existence, with all its trials and difficulties. We pattern our life on that of Christ, who said to seek first the kingdom of God and his justice. There are many temptations in this world. The devil tries to lure us away from our primary commitment to the realm of the spirit. We believe that one day we will share in the resurrection of Christ, and it is this faith that enables us to keep going and to sustain the sufferings of this wicked world.

St. Paul tells us that our faith is built on belief in the afterlife, and that if Christ did not rise, then our faith is in vain. In one sense, our belief in a life hereafter depends on the reality of Christ's own life hereafter. We know he rose on the third day, and we know that he is God and does not deceive us. So we are willing to put our lives on the block, so to speak, to lose out on the transient, imperfect pleasures of this life in order to gain the real happiness of the future life.

✳ YES

It is one thing to believe in the resurrection, and it is quite another thing to neglect one's present responsibilities. Living without reference to the actualities of one's life in the hope of being rewarded for this flight from reality is simply delusion. The Church's mistake has been to neglect the present under the illusion that in this way we prepare for eternal life.

Many people forget that Christ is still with us, and that we each have a responsibility to fulfill the promise of our creation. Christ sent us forth to establish the kingdom. And the kingdom is not a nebulous habitat somewhere on the other side of the grave. Scriptural scholars are adamant in insisting that Christ's kingdom is those who believe and who love here on earth.

To strive after happiness in the next life makes one puritanical and stoical. It stifles one's zest for living. I think Christ wants mankind to be happy in his work here on earth.

2. IS DEATH THE END OF LIFE?

§ *NO*

Death is not the end of life. Death is the beginning of life for us, eternal life in which we will receive the rewards of a life spent in the service of God or, if such was our will, the punishment for a life misspent. In the preface of the Mass for the Dead we are told that in death, life is not taken away but is merely changed.

It is unclear what this new life will be like. Some tell us that heaven is a place of sheer bliss. St. Thomas speaks of the beatific vision, when we will contemplate the reality that is God and see him face to face. St. Paul says that whereas now we see through a glass darkly, then we will be bathed in the brightness of eternal light.

We know that the Blessed Virgin was assumed bodily into heaven. She appeared at Lourdes and Fatima emanating the brilliance that we can expect for ourselves in heaven. The saints have also revealed to us the happiness that exists in heaven. One has only to read the revelation of Catherine Anne Emmerich to know about life on the other side of the grave.

❋ YES

When the first cosmonaut went into space, he is supposed to have made the remark that he did not find any signs of heaven or a God. His remark was indicative less of insolence than of reality. He was emphasizing the great strides man has made and the great future he has before him. Death is the only end we know. I like to look on it as a deadline. I know very little about life after death. I presume it will occur in one way or another; whether as reincarnation or whether as a happy hunting ground makes little difference to me. I prefer not to think about life after death because it takes my mind off the present life, which is really my concern.

It's odd how easily people forget Christ's parable of the man and his talent. The man hid his talent in the ground, and his master rebuked him for it. He was taking care of number one; he had to have his insurance policy, and as a result he frittered away his opportunity. This is what I think is wrong with the emphasis on death as the beginning of a new life.

Catholics make their religion morbid with all their emphasis on death. I remember once seeing in *Life* magazine a gruesome collection of skulls and skeletons that is supposedly the pride and joy of a Capuchin church in Rome. Tourists come from all over the world to feast their eyes on this macabre sight. The practices during Lent are especially dour. The imposition of ashes, the purple vestments, and the fasting all seem to indicate a sadistic delight in the reality of death.

I like to think of my religion as a cause of joy, a work of happiness. If the resurrection is a reality, then I know that my joy no man will take from me. This is true because I try to make my life not a death to the world, but a vibrant kindling source of happiness for myself and my fellow man. As St. Philip Neri is said to have remarked, May the Lord preserve us from sour saints!

3. DO YOU BELIEVE IN HELL?

§ YES

Hell is a state where the damned are sent because of grievous offenses against God. Hell is where God, the source of love and benediction, is not present. Hell is a nonconsuming fire, the torment of Dante's immortal "Inferno." In hell the damned are condemned for all eternity to a life of pain, sorrow, and misery. The greatest suffering for them is the realization that their damnation would not have happened if they had listened to the Church. The Church pleaded with them, gave them every opportunity, through the priests and the sacraments, to repent. But hardened sinners would not heed. They cursed and reviled the sacred appeals of the Church. And now they are enduring the penalty of their indifference and their arrogance. I have no pity for those who are in hell, for they had the opportunity to save themselves but thought they were better and wiser than God and the Church. Now they are paying for their foolishness.

Hell is a terrible reality that I live with every day. I am not sure that I will have the grace of final perseverance, since that is a special grace that no one can merit. I never want to go to hell, and so I make sure that my soul is always in the state of grace. If I happen to fall into what I think is mortal sin, I immediately say an Act of Contrition, then try to reach a priest to give me absolution. The thought of hell is a very salutary one and helps keep me on the straight and narrow.

✳ NO

The hell described as eternal punishment is not real. I can't believe that God would send a person to such a place forever and ever. It makes a mockery of the whole plan of creation. It smacks more of a medieval horror story than anything else. Less civilized generations in the past, especially those that made the Inquisition a way of life, could easily conjure up a God who would be so heartless and cruel. Religion and pain were easily associated, especially if you were on the wrong side of the communion rail.

Even if one were to grant the possibility of such an inhuman state as hell, how can one be sure that anyone is condemned to it? I doubt that Judas is in hell. God is so good and so forgiving that it would be out of character not to give a person another chance. If we understand the nature of mortal sin, we find that it is almost impossible to commit one. That is, who can ever be sure that he made an absolutely free choice between God and evil? And if he did, in a moment of madness, then how could he be culpable?

Moreover, how much time is needed to repent—a split second? We are progressing so rapidly in psychology and the behavioral sciences that the more we understand about man and his actions, the more we realize how impenetrable is the mind of man. Who can judge the motives of a person in a given action? Who can account for the influence of circumstances, and so on? I admit that God is capable of punishing, as he proved in the Old Testament, but not a lasting, devastating blow against a person for one moment of madness or weakness.

4. DO YOU BELIEVE IN PURGATORY?

§ YES

The Church's belief in purgatory reveals much about its outlook on life and this world. Purgatory is a place or a state in which the souls of the departed are forced to remain for a temporary period in order to remit the punishment due for their sins. This state, although it seems quite negative, is actually a sign of our Father's great love for his children. How many agnostics point a disbelieving and suspicious finger at God and say how cruel he is to condemn sinners to hell! They blithely throw out the notion of sin and ask how a just God could punish his creatures for all eternity because they failed once or twice. But in the same breath these very critics laugh scornfully when the doctrine of purgatory is presented.

God our Father does love us, and at the same time he is the

strictest of judges. He does reward some souls with heaven, and he does send other souls into the eternal pains of hell. But in his great kindness and mercy, he has created a place that saves many souls from the fires of never-ending damnation. This place—purgatory—is for those who have sinned and been forgiven, but who still have the effects of sin on their souls. These souls actually deserve hell, for they have rejected the love of God. But purgatory cleanses their souls and grants them a second chance to get into heaven.

In spite of fierce criticism, the Church has always held onto its doctrine of purgatory. People today claim that the Church holds extreme views, views that most people would reject. Yet this great doctrine of purgatory is an example of moderation. The Church's constant stand on this matter is a sure sign of its truth and moderation.

Purgatory is, of course, a state of punishment, and is most certainly not something to look forward to. The souls that are in purgatory are suffering horribly. What this suffering is would be hard to say. It has been pictured as fire, burning off the shameful effects of sinful life. Basically, though, the Church teaches that purgatory is a separation from God. This is suffering indeed. After all, a good Catholic spends his whole life preparing for his meeting with God at death, and then he finds himself forced to wait even longer before he can see him face to face. Even a person who has seen the terror of a child lost and separated from his father cannot appreciate one small fraction of the agony felt by a soul in purgatory.

The Church in its goodness has given us aids to avoid this pain of separation. Indulgences, prayers, offerings, all can help reduce the time we must spend in purgatory. We can apply these prayers to the souls already in purgatory; in fact, this is one of the great spiritual works of mercy. All Soul's Day is a special day set aside for this work of love.

Our whole life is simply a preparation for our meeting with God at death. It is as if we are in the womb until we are born unto God. We must constantly be alert to methods of ensuring that purgatory will be simply a brief stopping-off place before we arrive at our eternal destination, heaven.

✳ NO

The idea of purgatory is one more page in the Catholic mythology, one more symptom of the malaise that has afflicted Christianity almost from the start.

Why do people become Catholics? Why do they spend their whole lives trying to do good? One hears a great deal of talk in Catholic circles about the childlike qualities they are taught to exhibit. I think that the Church does teach a childlike religion. Like a little boy who is always seeking his parents' approval for his actions, the typical Catholic always has one eye looking upward to see if the fatherly Catholic God will seal his action with an approving smile. If the action is approved, the person will be rewarded. If not, some kind of punishment will be forthcoming. This reward-punishment syndrome, which has been discussed widely by modern psychologists, is becoming less and less effective as a tool for molding behavior. And a tool is just what it is! It is used to hammer minds into "proper," that is, programmed, types of action. For the Church, purgatory is one of these tools.

For the modern man the reward-punishment approach is obnoxious. The Church has to rethink its approach to morals and ethics. Is the life hereafter the reward or punishment of life on earth? Is life on earth simply a testing ground for fitness in eternal life? Why should Catholics be good? Just because the Church will approve? Because God will approve and reward the good Catholic? That seems such a shallow and selfish approach. Has the Church ever taught that we should do good just because it is right? Has the Church ever taught that we must do what we consider good even in the face of opposition from the Church herself? Although it has taught the supremacy of conscience in theory, has it ever allowed it in practice? What is good anyway? Can the Church tell the whole world what is right and what is not right? Each person must find his truth and pursue it, without regard to fear tactics such as threats of damnation.

What would happen if the Church were shown not to be the "sure winner," the only proclaimer of truth, as it professes to be? How many people would remain Catholics? How many people would seek some other "sure winner," another system that would guarantee security? The person who is more concerned about the right of truth than the might of approval—even from the Church —will have little time or patience for thoughts about the Damocles sword supposedly hanging over our heads: purgatory.

5. CAN ONE MERIT ETERNAL LIFE?

§ YES

This is the reason that justifies the regimen of the Catholic. He follows the rules, performs sacrifices, does without things, and in general mortifies the flesh so that he may be happy in heaven with God and the saints. If he were unable to merit eternal life, he would not be so fastidious and exacting. Of course, we have to define the word "merit." Strictly speaking, no one can merit eternal life. This is salvation, and as such, it is a gift of God. We are speaking very loosely when we say one can merit heaven. If a man fulfills his part of the bargain, the Church tells him that he has a better chance of obtaining a pass through the pearly gates than if he were to live a profligate and degenerate life. In a sense, a Catholic is gambling. But a gamble on the reputation of the Church is like an investment with Lloyds of London.

Many of the new theologians are doing a lot of damage by de-emphasizing merit. They are trying to take away this sense of security and sow doubts in the minds of many people. The fact that so many practices of the old Church have been abandoned —novenas, frequent penance and mortification, private devotion to the Eucharist—is making older people nervous. They are beginning to wonder if they have not been deluded and have been betting on a lame horse. This is why so many of the older generation are leaning more and more on the statements of Pope Paul, for they know that it is only from Rome that they can get the truth.

❋ NO

Insistence on the notion of merit makes religion a game. The idea of indulgences and the entire concept of merit has been a scandal to those outside the Church. Under this barter system, good deeds were made mechanical and inhuman.

One person compared the merit system to the Boy Scout program! For every good deed, you get a little badge. Just so, people perform acts of charity not because of need, but in the hope that they will get a reward. I often was told to "offer up" some difficulty, so that in this way I would gain a more splendiferous crown in heaven. Children used to argue about who would be higher in heaven. Christ reprimanded the Apostles for doing the same thing. Religion, then, is reduced to basic self-interest, and altruism for its own sake is destroyed.

The idea of spiritual bouquets is an offshoot of the merit system. Besides hoarding a drawer filled with your own spiritual gold, you can apply to another person the merit from your prayers and communions. The spiritual is estimated at a price. Then, too, there are Mass stipends. I know people who have five hundred dollars put aside for Masses after their death. They figure that they'll only have to stay a short time in purgatory, or not at all, if this money is used for Masses for the repose of their soul. This is a type of spiritual greed, and symptomatic of the "Jesus and ME" spirituality that preceded Vatican II.

Instead of gambling on my eternal happiness by following a set of rules and regulations, I would rather find God here on earth in my needy brother, and so fulfill the law. If God is no stranger to me here on earth, I doubt that he will fail to recognize me when he sees me face to face.

6. WILL THE WORLD COME TO AN END?

§ YES

Everything in the universe exists within the temporal sphere. All creation has a beginning, and it will have an end. Only God is eternal, without beginning or end. The end of the world is a very important doctrine in the Church's eschatology. Eschatology is the study of the "end time," of "last things." This belief concerning the end of the world is intimately connected with the final judgment of God.

The ancient Hebrews spoke of the "Day of the Lord." They feared that day of judgment when the world would be destroyed by fire. Christ spoke vividly about this day of awe when people should fear for their salvation. He spoke of the fire that will envelop the world at the end of time and depicted the scene of the Last Judgment when the sheep (the flock that has truly followed the God-Shepherd, Christ) will be on God's right side and the goats will be on his left.

Christ also spoke in parable about our need to be prepared for the Last Judgment. The parable of the ten virgins is an example of this. Some were ready for the "bridegroom," and others were not. Those who were late were refused entrance into the kingdom. The "bridegroom," of course, is Christ, who has promised that he will come again in glory. Just as there are signs of the coming of spring, so too will there be signs to predict the second coming of Christ. The Church lovingly keeps these thoughts in our minds and hearts through the liturgy especially on the last Sunday of Pentecost and the days of Advent. "Come, Lord Jesus" is the cry of the future-conscious Catholic.

This cry has been heard throughout the history of the Church. When Christ rose from the dead, he promised that he would return in glory. The early followers of Christ expected this second coming right away, so they tried to prepare themselves totally. They led mortified and secluded lives; they refused to marry or procreate. St. Paul had to warn them against extremes of this sort but even he felt that the Lord's return would be soon.

God works in strange ways. The world is nothing; it is temporary and transitory; we are pilgrims and travelers. Yet God has willed, in his infinite and mysterious love, to keep us here on earth for an indefinite period. We yearn to be rid of the yoke of the flesh. We earnestly await the awesome and glorious coming of the resurrected Christ. Yet we are in exile still. The end of this world—this so-often wicked world—is not only a doctrine of the Church, but also the blessed hope of its members.

✳ NO

The doctrine of the end of the world is a part of a general Church attitude against everything physical, everything material, everything of the flesh. It is a doctrine that was formulated long before the idea of evolution became known. The Church is only now beginning to accept the idea of evolution, much less the consequences of evolutionary theories. Only fifteen or twenty years ago the Church scornfully rejected the teachings of Teilhard de Chardin, the famous priest and scientist. Now he is accepted more than before, but most Church leaders have no idea of where such "radical" ideas will bring the Church.

I compare the life of the world with an individual's life. Who has not experienced the learning process of growing? Who has not arrived at various important stages of his life and realized that from that point there was no returning to past ways? Who has not experienced the many little and great "flashes" that bring unimagined enlightenment? Such life movements actually make one a new person. We can almost say that his previous life has ended. But, in fact, it is the same person with new ideas. It is a type of evolution, of growing, of expanding.

I believe that the world grows in the same way. Collectively, societies reach points that had previously been unimaginable. This became true in the scientific world when Copernicus proved that the sun, and not the earth, is the center of our universe. It was shown in the technological world when doctors said that the human body could not tolerate speeds over thirty-five miles an hour and then came locomotives chugging into the station at forty miles an hour. And it has happened many times in the moral world. It occurred when Zoroaster, a religious leader in Persia in the sixth century B.C., said, "If others are good to me, I am good to others. If others are bad to me, I am still good to them. Thus all will become good." Here we have the first expression of the golden rule. It moved man to a level of ethics that had not been considered before.

Another level was reached when Jesus proclaimed his message of life and salvation for all men. Men had never before received such a challenge, such a mission. Christ's call gave us unheard-of heights at which to shoot. But I believe that the world will continually move on to new "flashes." Like the mature person who hopes never to reach a point where there are no more mountains to climb, no more challenges to encounter, the world should constantly be on the alert to receive new and evolutionary influences.

The Church generally frowns on such searching, since it claims to possess the truth in its fullness. The doctrine of the end of the world proclaims that the time will come when true and eternal reality will take over from the false and illusory existence of the world. I think, rather, that the world will continue to grasp more and more of the reality that it was given by God until it is fulfilled in truth. Completed, fulfilled—not destroyed. We must set our vision on building and fulfilling the purpose of this world rather than set the sights of our destructive doctrinal guns on a very challenging universe.

7. DO YOU BELIEVE IN FATE?

§ YES

I believe in fate, but not pure chance. We've been taught to believe that there is nothing that does not have a reason. Even the most seemingly absurd event, the most horrible and senseless crime, are not without purpose. This is indeed a mystery not to be understood by us in this life. But we must accept this truth on faith: Our lives are not ruled by pure chance, but by the fatherly hand of God.

I believe in fate, but not in predestination. The Church has officially condemned the heresy of predestination. This heresy was a very important part of the Protestant revolt. Calvin claimed that we cannot be redeemed by our own merits, so we are either saved or not saved. Either way, we can do nothing about it. I believe that we cannot merit salvation completely on our own, but that we can affect the outcome of our lives and, with the help of God's grace, put ourselves in a position of advantage on Judgment Day.

Predestination is an evil and pernicious heresy. I don't believe in that kind of fate. But I do believe in the kind of fate that the Church calls divine providence. Basically, our belief in divine providence stems from our knowledge that God has a plan of salvation for the world. This plan, which finds its fulfillment in Christ, affects every moment and every aspect of my life on earth. God is personally involved in all my concerns. He will never let evil hurt me, because I am his child, and he is goodness itself. He will work everything for my good, even the apparently absurd and useless happenings. This loving care does not coerce me in any way. I am still free to spurn his love. I am still able to remain what I am, a lowly sinner. But I rest consoled in the fact that God demonstrates his great love for me through his divine providence. God's love is the greatest influence on my life.

✳ NO

In my mind dependence on fate or providence is a resignation from the world. People who try to force others to accept these magical mysteries are unable to face the reality of their existence. What is the reality? Mainly absurdity. So much in life doesn't make sense. This is what many of our great (and many of the not-so-great) writers have been speaking about in the theater and literature of the absurd. I can feel a good deal of sympathy with such writers. What can be more absurd than to have one's life snuffed out in the shattered wreck of a moving metal monster— the automobile? Who can explain the death of a baby who was playing with a plastic laundry bag? Why does a soldier die at the hand of a complete stranger? Who can explain the ultimate horror, the hydrogen bomb, which can destroy, in minutes, the work of centuries?

These literally are life-and-death questions. They have no answers. Completely unexplainable, totally useless, the absurd forces us to temper our idealistic outlook on life. We must learn to live in spite of absurdity. Why do I say this so blithely? Because I have tried to evaluate the realities of my life. I see no evidence of God's influence in my daily life or in anyone else's. I don't think that God has it in his plan to interfere in our lives. The Church cannot say that God gives everything a purpose and then admit to the reality of a woman who has lost her husband in World War II and her only son in Vietnam. *There is no reason for such sorrow.*

Man can make himself master of his destiny. He cannot find purpose in these absurd events, but he can find purpose in spite of them. He is a *tabula rasa*—a blank page that he alone can write on. He can give himself a purpose, or he can surrender to the absurd. But in either case he will not be like those who cover their fear of life with the "Linus blanket" of a predestination philosophy. The Church dictates what all men should be, and in this way saves the individual from having to make the radical life decisions his existence demands.

We must reject this "man-is-an-acorn-he-must-grow-into-an oak" theory. The world today is so complex, and societies are so varied, that it is unrealistic to force an essential character and purpose on man. Man is not tied to or bound by any purpose. He must create his own goals, his own essence. Only then can he be considered master of his destiny. Only when he has faced the many meaningless things on earth can he find meaning in his own existence. A person who is in control of his own life has no undue fear of outside events that he cannot control. His life can still be snuffed out without reason, but he accepts this possibility. He doesn't overly fear death, because he knows it will come no matter what, and because he is living his life to the hilt now. A man must find his own purpose in life. He must not allow himself to be ruled by outside influences, whether these influences be called divine providence or absurdity. Man can rule himself. He has been put in this world, and it is the only home he knows. Man possesses the absurdity of freedom.

8. DO YOU ACCEPT CAPITAL PUNISHMENT?

§ YES

Capital punishment is a deterrent against further crime, not only in the case of the condemned individual, but also for others, who are made to realize that man cannot take another's life with impunity. Statistics show that in those areas where the death penalty is not legal the incidence of crime is greater. In our own decade the number of major violations against law and order has increased. Multiple murders are the unique badge of our day. I see this disregard for life and law as the direct result of those who would spare the rod and spoil the child. In the Bible we are taught that society has the right to demand an eye for an eye, a tooth for a tooth. A person who takes another's life has invaded a sacred area, and he must be punished. If he is allowed to keep his own life, chances are that he will be paroled in a short time, and again let loose on society. Society must protect itself.

There is no religious contradiction in supporting the concept of capital punishment. Religion elevates the dignity of man and consecrates the worth of his life. It thus follows that religion would support capital punishment. The Fifth Commandment says, "Thou shalt not kill," but in cases of self-defense and for the protection of life and limb a person may take another's life, as he may in the case of war.

Capital punishment is society's way of defending itself against the morally sick. As the representative of God in the community, society has the right to take life if it is in the interests of the common good. And allowing a half-crazed killer to escape punishment is definitely a violation of the common good.

❋ *NO*

Capital punishment is senseless and is sheer murder. As one lawyer put it, he is against murder whether committed by one person or a jury of twelve. Capital punishment violates the very nature of man, because it assumes that there can be no reasonable doubt as to the culpability of the accused person. Moreover, it shuts off any hope of repentance or correction. The horror of it is that even after a careful trial, there have been cases when the wrong person was convicted of a crime. Often it was too late to make amends, for the person had already been executed. I don't think man has the right to take another's life except in a legitimate case of self-defense.

Society is certainly not God. It may have authority that comes from God, but that doesn't make it God. Society does not give life, therefore it has no right to take it away. The common good is protected when the individual who violated the law is taken out of the ranks of society. Then society must do all in its power to help rehabilitate that person. Modern penology has shown that capital punishment is hardly a deterrent to serious crime. Crime must be attacked at its root causes, which are poverty, discrimination, and substandard education. Crime must be prevented. All capital punishment accomplishes is to lock the barn after the horse has been stolen.

Religious people often seem to forget the words of Jesus in the story of the woman taken in adultery: "Let him who is without sin cast the first stone." This is why I am against capital punishment.

9. DO YOU BELIEVE IN PARAPSYCHOLOGICAL EXPERIENCES?

§ *NO*

I believe very strongly in the spiritual realm, but I have no patience with ghosts and spiritualism, haunted houses, and other superstitious things. I think I am acting in accord with the Church. Those who believe in such things are dangerous. They are like the flying-saucer people; they have nothing better to do than to go around scaring people. They don't have a true idea about what life is. I think such people are quite a bit like the primitive people in Africa or Latin America. I read in *Mission* magazine about their superstitious practices of praying to wooden dolls and dancing wildly. Such actions are bad enough in primitive cultures, but to see the same attitudes in supposedly educated people makes me wonder about their common sense and sanity.

The Church believes very strongly in life after death. It also solemnly declares that persons who have died can have a miraculous influence on the world. But this influence is altogether different from the superstitious practices of the so-called parapsychologists. The influence of the Blessed Virgin and the saints is supernatural. It's conditioned by faith; we have faith in the infallible divine revelation of God. Others have nothing but their own imaginations.

The Church, in its constant and loving defense of the truth, has always been meticulous in assuring itself, and anyone else who is open enough to accept its word on faith, that miraculous occurrences are truly supernatural and not just the overflow of someone's neurotic imagination. Only when the Church fully recognizes an event as supernatural can we accept it as real. Unless we are willing to determine our judgment in the light of the Church's evaluation, we can easily be misled into purely fanciful beliefs. Parapsychological experiences reflect an antireligious, antifaith direction. True children of God should shun such superstition.

❋ YES

I have a tremendous respect for the great variety of experiences in this world. One can get an idea of varied cultures and life styles just by visiting another state in this country. If people who live in the same country can have such different experiences, how wide a range of influences must affect people throughout the world. I am constantly awed by the tremendous possibilities I find in this world, and so I refuse to rule out any plausible experience.

If I respect the varied experiences, I respect even more the people who have experienced them. I give myself a great deal of credit for thoughtfulness and discernment. If I demand from others what I give myself, can I deny that respect when others demand it of me? Besides, who am I to judge another's experience? If he has truly experienced it, it is real for him, and who am I to contradict him?

As to parapsychological experiences specifically, there is a great deal of scientific investigation going on right now. Duke University is famous for its methodological approach to these experiences. University researchers have been working for years on cases that stun the imagination. Yet they do not reject such happenings as the haunted house on Long Island as purely figments of the imagination.

Ten years ago the realms of outer space were completely unknown. Today, through diligent and expensive research much is known about the territory beyond the earth. We know very little, however, about "inner space." Who knows what the mind is capable of? How can anyone condemn ESP (extrasensory perception) when very few know anything about the subject?

I believe that we are entering on the most important phase of human investigation: the powers of the mind. Because we know very little about the mind, we tend to fear what discoveries might be made. That is why conservative organizations and many people in the Church oppose such research. But we must always truly desire new knowledge. Although the Church often comes across as the savior who knows it all, it is often most ignorant on subjects it fears. The fact that people have claimed parapsychological experiences means that such experiences are a possibility. We must not close them off without a real test.

10. DO YOU BELIEVE IN EUTHANASIA (MERCY KILLING)?

§ NO

One of the great features of Catholic belief is that it helps one approach complicated problems in a methodological and consistent way. Thus, the Church has many firm and irreversible principles, and all the good Catholic has to do is apply them to his practical, concrete situation. If he does this, the answer will be readily available although its application might not be so simple. Without the Church, many of these problems would be solved, not according to principle, but according to practical, natural reason alone. Pragmatism is a great danger, and the Church alone can save us from it.

An example might help explain why pragmatism is so evil. According to many practical theorists euthanasia in some cases is not only legal, but a work of mercy. Now, it is one of the most basic principles of any moral code that killing is wrong. To take the life of a person without sufficient and just cause is completely immoral. Even the person himself is not allowed to take his life.

But according the pragmatist, mercy killing is sometimes proper. In the beautiful moral code of Catholicism, euthanasia is properly classified for what it is: a prostitution of the plan of God. In God's plan, life is meant to be a severe preparation for the true life after death. God does not want anyone to cut that preparation short. Pragmatists claim that if a person is suffering and wants to die, he should be allowed that freedom of choice. But the Church states that suffering is one of the most important means of preparing for heaven. Christ, our loving Saviour, suffered. God gave life to us; only God can take it away. Men must not act like God!

The Church cannot change its belief in the sacredness of life. Practical issues are not involved. It is the principle that counts, no matter what.

✳ YES

Many people are against euthanasia because they are afraid it will be abused. I am just as much against the abuse as they are. But I am *for* its proper use. Man is master of his destiny in most instances. He should have control over his life. If he is at a point in life where there is no future for him, where he is suffering intensely and his suffering is leading him to a slow death, I believe he should have the right to decide if he wishes the ultimate relief. This is a decision of the highest magnitude, of course. It requires the greatest clarity of insight and judgment. But that doesn't mean that such a decision should not be made.

No one else can make this decision for the person. If anyone had made such a decision for Helen Keller when she was a child, millions of people would have been deprived of her marvelous inspiration of courage. The same is true of many great musicians and artists who were born with various defects. Only the person himself should have this right over his own life.

Euthanasia is by no means a disrespect for life. Rather, it is a denial of the very disrespectful view that looks on life as a mere experiment and preparation for the future life in heaven. When life reaches that point when nothing more can be gained and much can be lost, then life is not keeping its promise. I feel that the person who is living that life should be allowed to make an honest decision about terminating it.

The problems of mercy killing are difficult and complex. Objective and high-sounding moral principles will not provide easy answers, no matter what the Church's claim. It is easy to say that people like myself have no morals or principles at all if we don't have the morals and principles of the Catholic Church. It is easy to say, but it is not true. I live by principles. I am interested in principles that speak about the real world, not some super realm that exists only in the minds of holier-than-thou people. I believe in mercy killing because I believe in mercy!

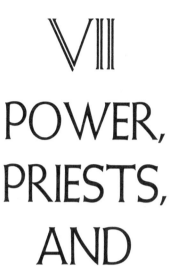

VII

POWER, PRIESTS, AND PARISHES

When Pope Paul visited the United Nations the American people went wild. It was a distinct honor for our country, especially since this was the first time in history that a Pope had ever set foot on American soil.

Why is the Pope such an important figure in a country where Catholics number barely one-fifth of the total population? One might say that although America is not a Catholic country, the Catholics it does have are quite vocal. Catholics in America have a unique reverence for Rome and the Pope. Inside ecclesiastical circles *romanitas* is a virtue, a suave know-how. And whatever issues from Rome is best expressed in the ancient Augustinian dictum: *Roma locuta est, causa finita est*. "Rome has spoken. The case is decided."

"Pope," "Rome," and "bishop" are words consecrated in dignity and uttered in deep reverential fear. One way to put a convent or rectory into a frenzy is to announce that the bishop will be at the front door in five minutes.

In the priest, too, we significantly experience the Church and all it stands for. How many people have turned away from the Church in bitterness because of something a particular priest has done to them?

Priests are in the news today. They are leaving the priesthood in droves. Those who remain seem to be organizing, and there is even a priest's union. Many of them are rebelling against celibacy. Have you ever considered the consequences of a married clergy?

Are you envious of the young priest, barely twenty-six or twenty-seven years old, who has his own car, no family responsibilities, and a seemingly unlimited source of pocket money provided by the Mass stipend system and the "Please say a prayer for me, Father" syndrome? How many people can afford to retire so early in life? Do you think, then, that the Church should abolish the clerical estate and introduce worker-priests?

Vocations to the priesthood are way down. Young people fight the idea of secluded seminaries and irrelevant theology courses. They term the seminary discipline unrealistic. What are your ideas on seminary training?

How many people are in your parish? Three thousand families? You have Mass every Sunday on the hour, and the Church is packed. Do you know these people personally? Do you think a parish can operate effectively as a unit if it is so sprawling and large?

If you look upon religion as a service, then you seldom pay much attention, if any, to the structure and personnel that provide the service—just as you don't pay much attention to the messenger who delivers your telegrams or the linen-service man who provides your clean sheets.

Should you consider religion a service, or are you short-changing yourself? Because the fact is that religion is not a service, it is a way of life, a life style. Therefore, you cannot afford to ignore the people within the Church structure. To do so is to overlook the reality of these people. They do touch your life, and they do help determine your future for better or for worse. This discussion, then, touches the heart of many problems in your own life. It deals with issues that you should think about.

1. DO YOU ACCEPT THE ROLE OF THE POPE IN YOUR LIFE?

§ YES

The Pope represents security and orthodoxy. He is the Vicar of Christ on earth. When he speaks, it is Christ speaking. Take away the Pope and the Catholic religion fails.

I believe in the infallibility of the Pope. I know that when he makes an *ex cathedra* statement it is carefully prepared and thought out in the light of the Tradition of the Church and the inspired writings of the Scriptures. I place my complete confidence in the Pope, since he combines the best of human knowledge with the divine assurance of infallibility. He cannot make a mistake in matters of faith and morals.

The Pope symbolizes the Good Shepherd. It is tragic that the Church is so torn by division and confusion. The dissension must be a heavy burden on the Holy Father. At Fatima, Our Lady said that the Holy Father would have much to suffer, and now he is really going through a Gethsemane. He is trying hard to keep the Church together during this storm. We need the Holy Father as never before. And he in turn needs us and our loyalty.

✳ NO

I honestly do not understand the role of the Pope in my life. I do not see the need for him, as a figurehead. Hans Küng has written a book in which he shows that historically the churches of Rome and Antioch got along quite well together even though they were not headed by one person. He also shows that many of the statements of the Council of Trent reveal a historical vacuum, and are not genuinely based in theology. I love Pope Paul and I think he is a great man who is suffering. But I don't see the necessity of a medieval prince set over me. I don't see his office as compatible with that of Peter and Paul, who exercised their authority as humble men and who were not surrounded with pomp and splendor. Vatican City, with its functionaries and its Mercedes Benz parking lot, its riches and its art treasures, is a genuine scandal.

The Pope rules over an impossible kingdom, made up of varying and opposing ideologies. If there cannot be one nation politically, how can there be harmony in the great intangibles of religion?

Many of Pope Paul's statements are ill-advised, for he is making official pronouncements that only cause people to turn away from him. He may be well intentioned, but as a religious leader he exercises no influence over me. Yet the organization of the Church is such that he is given great power over me, deciding what is mortal sin and what is not, and thereby supposedly jeopardizing my eternity. I don't blame people for not accepting his decision on the pill. Why should they?

2. DO YOU ACCEPT ROME'S INFLUENCE IN YOUR LIFE?

§ YES

Rome is the Eternal City and the home of the Pope. Rome is the seat of the government of the Church where thousands of good priests and sisters help the Pope run the vast empire of Catholicism. The Pope appoints most of the persons who help him govern, and therefore I see their words and actions as reflecting the will of the Holy Father. That is why I always accept the decision of Rome on anything.

I always side with Rome, as in the case of the Immaculate Heart of Mary sisters. When Rome tells the sisters to obey their cardinal and start wearing religious habits again, so to stop causing scandal, I don't know why the sisters persist in fighting.

Rome represents the will of God to me. I cannot imagine, as some try to tell me, that politics is played in Rome, that there are decisions attributed to the Pope of which he has no knowledge. The Church is a spiritual organization, and I refuse to associate the wheeling and dealing of politics with the ecclesiastical government. People tell me there are scandals in Rome among the functionaries, but I find it hard to believe that the Church of God would be infested with agents of the devil. I find that the people who are so quick to criticize Rome do not understand a thing about the intricacies of Church government.

Someone tried to tell me that the revolt of the bishops at Vatican II signaled the end of the Roman Curia and other offices in Rome. I find this hard to believe since the Pope was at the council too and would never allow disunity to triumph. The priests in Rome are so intelligent and so dedicated that they are a credit to the Holy Father. I only wonder why more of them don't challenge modern theologians to discuss the true points of Christianity.

✳ *NO*

Rome has emerged as a power in the Catholic Church because of historical circumstances. As it stands now the papacy is
usually accorded to an Italian, despite the fact that Vatican City
is supposed to be an international state without political attach-
ment to Italy. The government of the Church has been for too
long the exclusive property of the Italians. And as often happens
when an international organization is dominated by one nation,
the Church has suffered immeasurably from her singular attach-
ment to the Italian base. I think that the greatest single victory
of Vatican II was the exposure of the shallow leadership exercised
by the Roman Curia and the dictatorship they represented. More
than that, Vatican II forced the Pope to expand the membership
of the various religious offices to include people of other races
and nationalities.

It was only the second Vatican Council that saved the
Church. There is an expression in Rome to the effect that the
laws of the Church are made in Rome and exported for observance. The Italian Church has never been worthy of emulation.
When the race was on for filled churches and long confessional
lines, Italy did not make a handsome showing. Now that the
Church is being renewed the hard-nosed reactionaries are the
Italians who for so long dictated policy but did not observe it.
Now they find that people are not frightened by the tactics and
politics of Rome, that they can distinguish these from the truths
necessary for salvation.

3. D O   Y O U   S E E   A   R O L E   F O R
   T H E   B I S H O P   I N   Y O U R   L I F E ?

§ *YES*

The bishop is the spiritual descendant of the Apostles. He is
one of the apostolic band, and he helps the Pope in the ruling
of the Church. He is empowered to teach and to save. He is in

charge of a portion of the Church called a diocese, and he is directly responsible to the Pope for the spiritual conduct of those committed to his care. The bishop, then, is an important factor in the life of the Catholic, for he is the direct and immediate leader. The bishop instructs him in his faith, and he provides him with priests and sisters to help counsel him in his life struggle for salvation.

The bishop effects his work through the chancery office. Although I rarely see my bishop, I know that he is always there should I need him. He is busy with confirmations and personal visits throughout the diocese. The bishop is my father, and I feel honored to have a man of his intelligence and competence directing my pilgrimage to paradise. I have never spoken personally to the bishop, although I have been introduced to him and, of course, I see him often in the daily press. He is distant by nature of his office and by the burden of his extremely important duties.

I know that even non-Catholics look to the bishop for moral leadership, and I thank God and the Holy Father for giving us this gifted priest to help us in these troubled times. I pray daily for my bishop that God may sustain him and grant him length of days in the service of the Master.

❋ NO

I cannot feel close to the bishop of my diocese. To me he is just a distant executive who keeps the various segments of the diocese together. He is management and the priests are labor. The lay people are his commodity. Their support enables him to occupy himself with an office that is more prestigious than efficient. I cannot identify with him for he insists on dressing in the costume of a medieval prince. He lives by himself, and I seldom see him except at a distance, when he delivers a long and boring sermon. He usually drives a sleek black Cadillac, and I hear that he and other bishops spend much of the winter on the beaches of Florida. They are really high-priced executives who have been given the office of bishop because they are good moneymakers or good managers.

I seldom see the bishop with the people. I know a slum area

where there are thousands of poor people, some with barely enough to eat. I think Christ would be found there with them. But our bishop seldom goes there, except to pass through on his way to the airport.

I think the bishop we have is a nice gentleman, but I don't pay too much attention to his words or his actions, because they seldom remind me of Christ. He is famous for platitudes, and lots of priests don't dare go near him. He claims he is their father, but they can see him only by appointment. Perhaps he has too many functions to attend. Perhaps he is nothing but a figurehead. But if this is true, why do we support the sham? Why are we deceiving ourselves? Why can't the Church streamline itself? I think there is a place for a bishop of the caliber of Timothy or Paul. But those great men would feel ill at ease with our little princes and kings. The gap in understanding between the bishop and the flock is pathetic. I would rather have no bishop than the figurehead we have now, for then we wouldn't be hypocrites and the Church would be able to function more effectively.

4. DO YOU BELIEVE IN THE SEPARATION OF CHURCH AND STATE?

§   *NO*

I believe that to separate Church from state means to keep God out of the state. And that is precisely what has happened in America. The Supreme Court has legislated God out of the schools, so that now a youngster cannot even hear the name of God mentioned on school property. God is the founder of the state as well as of the Church. I can understand that there might be difficulties if the religion of the state were not the true religion. It is possible that this would mean persecution of the true religion. In this case, then, I would very much favor the separation of Church and state. But if the religion of the state is the true religion, as is the Catholic religion, then I think that the only right thing is to have Church and state united. I don't think the state should interfere unduly in the functions of the Church, such as demanding that it have a voice in the naming of bishops or dictating what should be taught in the schools. But where it would redound to the best interests of the Church, then I think the state should give every bit of cooperation requested by the officials of the Church.

Freedom of religion is a good thing so long as the true religion is not hurt. But I think the state has an obligation to see to it that all its subjects are protected from evil influences and that the Church is able, financially and with prestige, to fulfill its divine mission.

✳ YES

I do not see any justification for the union of Church and state. History and even contemporary dictatorships show the folly of a church united with a state. I can see a lot of advantages for a state religion, but I do not believe that the state has the right to violate the freedom of choice of individuals and force them to accept a religion against their will. I think that Vatican II, with the brilliant groundwork laid by John Courtney Murray, brought individual conscience into the forefront. We have much to thank God for in the acceptance of this document on religious liberty.

If the Church is aligned with the state, the possibility of corruption and collusion becomes great. In Italy, where Church and state are so friendly, there is a great infringement upon the intellectual freedom and expression of the people. Particularly in the area of intellectual freedom is harm possible from a unified Church and state.

In the United States religious groups have occasionally influenced government policy, as in the case of the Volstead Act, which prohibited the sale of alcoholic beverages. It didn't take the country long to realize it had been duped. Censorship in one form or another usually marks the unification of Church and state. Then begin the blacklistings and inquisitions and trials by association. All these were with us during the McCarthy era. And these could be with us again if we don't accept the practicality and freedom of the First Amendment.

5. DO YOU BELIEVE IN FREEDOM OF WORSHIP?

§ *NO*

Freedom necessarily implies that a person has adequate knowledge and understanding of his options. I don't think that anyone but the Pope and those associated with him are in a position to choose freely the kind of worship they want. No one could possibly understand all the choices available because there are just too many religions.

Some people want baptism deferred until the child reaches the age of reason and is able freely and responsibly to make the proper choice. I think that this is the height of foolishness. A child should be received into the religion of his parents, especially if that religion happens to be the true religion. To deny him that happiness and privilege simply because of his tender age is insidious and harmful. Suppose the youngster dies without baptism, as sometimes happens. Suppose a friend or a college education turns him away from any religion whatsoever. Should a good Catholic education be forfeited and spurned in the interest of freedom of worship?

I believe freedom of worship must be guaranteed in communist countries, where many unfortunate people are not permitted to worship God as they see fit. When the communists take over a country, the first thing they do is kill the priests and nuns, close down the Catholic schools, and jail as many Catholics as possible. They know that once they cut off true religion at the source, they can then carry out their takeover without much resistance.

The Church is the glory of our times and the hope of nations. Let those who seek freedom of worship ensure that freedom for our fellow Catholics who are denied this basic human right by the communist invaders. Let us pray that they may be strong in their faith and firm in their resolve in the face of persecution.

❋ YES

A person is free to worship God in any way he pleases. This freedom, besides being guaranteed by most enlightened nations, is basic to the human personality. You cannot force a person to accept your understanding of God and your particular response to the Gospel. You can share your insights and exemplify your beliefs through zealous action. But force and religion are not compatible. I think that even within a particular religious structure, such as Catholicism, the individual must be permitted wide scope.

If I choose to worship God as a Catholic, then I don't think anybody has the right to tell me how and when to worship him. That is why I think it is foolish to force people to go to Mass every Sunday under pain of mortal sin. It is also foolish to force a priest to read the psalms every day under pain of sin, or to make seminarians and nuns go to confession once a week and recite particular prayers at a given time every day of the year. This violates freedom of worship. It destroys spontaneity, which is of such great importance to a fulfilling God-relationship. I don't think you can force people to love, and worship surely is an expression of one's love of God and neighbor. Rubrics and laws are impositions, nothing more.

A person who really understands God will not have any difficulty finding the proper manner of worship. He may differ in manner from you or me, but we must respect his basic right to worship God according to his conscience. This is why I strongly believe the Catholic Church has a lot of catching up to do, even in understanding its own documents of Vatican II, especially the one on religious freedom.

6. DO YOU KNOW YOUR PARISH PRIESTS?

§ YES

There are four priests in my parish. Although I don't see them very often, I feel that I know them quite well. I know which one is devoted and which one simply gets out on the altar and does his job. One I seek out for confession, for he listens to me, is kind, and is not in a rush. As a result, people form lines outside his box. I never have any of the priests to my home for dinner. But I know that they do have their close circle of friends.

I don't think it is good to get too friendly with a priest. The relationship should be like that of doctor and patient. I like my personal physician but I never see him socially, because our relationship is strictly professional. Priests should relate to the parishioners in the same way. When priests become too familiar, they can become the subject of malicious gossip. They are on a pedestal, and they hurt their image by trying to be regular guys.

Priests should not let their humanity show. They are supposed to be a source of good example to us. It doesn't help when we hear they have similar or worse problems to contend with than we have. If a person is weak to begin with it can shake his faith in the Church. If a parishioner knows the priests too well, he might close his mind to their sermons. Priests belong in the sanctuary and in the sacristy, and not on the fairways and in the living room. If anticlericalism springs up, they'll have no one to blame but themselves.

❋ NO

I don't know many priests personally. I know quite a few "spoiled priests," fellows who have quit the seminary. I know one ex-priest. But that's about it. I think it is a shame that priests don't make themselves more available. I know there are many priests who visit the laity in their homes to socialize. I don't approve of this.

I look on a priest as another Christ, meaning that he is dedicated to the services of the Church. He belongs out in the marketplace, helping the poor and serving those who need the comfort and mercy of Christ. I hate the idea of a priest as a professional businessman who renders a service on weekends. Christ is the only priest, really, and men only share in his priesthood. The priest is supposed to be a leader and a teacher. He leads through constructive programs of self-help, and he teaches through good example and deeds.

Priests have many problems in being accepted in their own system. They have to wait years for responsibility, and most of them are treated like little boys. I can understand that with their years of training and education they would resent being regarded by their pastors and bishops as woodenheads. But they don't have to put up with this. They should abandon their celibate citadels and sanitized surroundings. They should put up store-front churches and hold the Eucharist in the stream of life. The priesthood is not failing; it is rather the priests who have let life pass them by. The loss of vocations is all to the good, because the caliber of priests should improve.

7. SHOULD PRIESTS GET INVOLVED IN SOCIAL ISSUES?

§ NO

I think priests should take care of bell, book, and candle. Organizations exist to meet social problems, and, to judge by the civil-rights legislation that is being shoved down our throats, they are doing a good job. The number of people on welfare is almost pathetic. When I was young, people were ashamed to go on relief. Now there are thousands who live a slothful life, collecting their government checks regularly. The dole is quite high and is an enticement to avoid work, for most people who are unskilled and uneducated can collect more from welfare than from honest labor.

Priests choose their way of life for a religious reason, and they should stay in the churches. Pius XII once stated that priests should get out of the sacristy and into the world, but by that I am sure he meant priests should get out and attract the people into church for Mass and confession.

Nothing annoys me more than to read stories like the one about Father Philip Berrigan, who poured blood all over the draft records in his city. Why a priest would destroy government property like that, I'll never understand. Father Groppi of Milwaukee is another one who annoys me. Priests like these give the others a bad name and ultimately bring dishonor to the priesthood. No wonder vocations are down. And then Father Kavanaugh going on television and stabbing the Church in the back. He told the Church to go to hell. What can we expect from our youth if this is the way priests act? Believe me, if priests don't start tending the store, contributions will be way down. That will get them where it hurts.

❋ YES

A person will answer this question on the basis of his own understanding of religion. If Catholicism is simply devotions, novenas, on-the-hour Mass, and long confessional lines, then naturally priests belong there and not out in the world. If Catholicism is a God-relationship, built on love and concern for one's fellow man, then the priest is practicing his religion when he shows leadership in social issues. If Catholics are discontented with priests' involvement in social issues, then their religion has failed. How can anyone read the Gospels and penetrate the mission of Christ without seeing that the death of religion is obsession with rites and ritualism? Priests have themselves failed in not becoming more involved in the great social questions. The Church has a tremendous social doctrine, but so much of it is dead-letter. Even the clergy doesn't take the Church seriously. Look at the criticism that followed *Pacem in terris* and more recently, Pope Paul's statement on the *Development of Nations*.

Priests are supposed to be leaders. The younger priests are disgusted with being glorified office boys and altar boys. They became priests to help people. Civil rights, discrimination, and poverty demand some type of involvement from those who claim to be Christ's messengers. The death of religion is intrinsically bound up with the apathy of priests. If people cannot read this handwriting on the wall, then they deserve to be passed by.

8.   ARE PARISHES TOO LARGE?

§   NO

It all depends on what you think a parish is for. We don't have enough parishes, and we are badly understaffed in those parishes we do have. What do you want to do? Cut the parishes into smaller units? Then you are simply aggravating the problem. This kind of thinking is typical of the wide-eyed liberal. He has all the answers on paper, but chances are he has never spent one hour in earnest conversation with those who know the problems of the parish.

According to a recent survey, only one-third of the total parish even go to church on a regular basis. If we split up the present parishes, then all we'll have is small units with the same problems. We'd have to multiply personnel and supplies, and this is impractical. There are not enough priests and nuns to go around. We already have huge schools, huge churches, and huge debts. Why should we abandon these and start parishes without proper facilities? In addition to the financial burden of starting new facilities, the abandoned facilities would have to be maintained.

Some people speak of regional schools and churches. But this is also impractical, because most parish structures were built on the basis of local population. As the population increased, new facilities were erected. The huge inner-city edifices that are like large mausoleums represent the evils of bad planning. Why duplicate this and dot the countryside with more ghost churches simply because someone has the bright idea that the Church would function better in smaller units? Planning is needed, as is an understanding of the vast financial burdens that are being assumed. Many schools are being vacated because there are not enough nuns to staff them. Do you want these to be staffed for regional needs? Where are we going to get the nuns? Until someone comes up with a proper plan, all this talk about smaller parishes is so much poppycock.

✳ YES

The present parishes are too large. Now if you think of religion as a business, then I would say don't change the present set-up, because finances and personnel are realistic problems. But if you think religion should fulfill the very reason of its being, then you should not tolerate the present financial burden for something that is completely useless. Why have huge building complexes and vast Sunday morning herdings if all this does not accomplish the will of Christ?

Catholicism is not having any realistic influence on the world today because it is not taken seriously. Our vast churches are filled on Sunday, but these people couldn't care less about the person kneeling next to them. They go to the communion rail together, but as soon as they rise they forget the intimate bond they have just forged. Many don't see religion as anything but a one-tone relationship with God.

Priests cannot cope with all the problems of a sprawling parish. The same is true of the schools. Catholicism doesn't even have a chance. What we need are smaller dioceses and smaller parishes where priests and people can get to know one another, and then are able to cooperate with one another in establishing a real Christian force. I opt for store-front churches.

9. DO YOU APPROVE OF THE WORKER-PRIEST CONCEPT?

§ NO

Priests should take care of their churches. Pope Pius XII squashed the worker-priests in France, and I think he did the right thing. These priests were working in factories under the pretext of converting the factory hands. Many abandoned the priesthood, and some actually became communists. They placed their faith in jeopardy by neglecting their religious duties. They gave up their breviaries and did not say Mass any more. It isn't too hard to see why their experiment failed. They tried to become workers, and lost their vocation. "Heresy of action" had taken over. Abandon your prayer life and God will leave you alone. The worker-priests seemed to think that the experience of history was useless. But the Pope knew the story, and put a stop to the fiasco before the idea started to gain support in other countries.

It is too bad that since Vatican II priests have been acting irresponsibly and trying to reactivate the notion of a worker-priest. A priest should work, but his work is already cut out for him as a minister of the Gospel. I cannot understand the young curates who feel that they have nothing to do all day. Why don't they go out and try to get people to go to church? Why don't they work on their sermons and try to improve them? Why don't they continue their studies or do research in theology?

Let priests spend more time in prayer so that God will give them the grace to redeem the hardened sinner. Let them spend more time in the confessional and less on the golf course. Then they won't be bored. Let priests be about their Father's business.

❊ YES

The present system has produced an elite class, the priesthood. Just go to confirmation or a Forty Hours devotion and you'll see a solemn procession of pious surpliced priests. But go around to the rectory about an hour after the service, and your eyes will be opened.

A priest has more time on his hands than he needs. He could set a good example if he went out and earned his bread. I don't think that hard work and sweat are incompatible with the priesthood. After all, Paul was a tentmaker and prided himself on not being a social parasite. The Church has long since lost the working man. The experiment in Paris was a good beginning. Now is the time to re-evaluate that experiment in the light of our contemporary situation and the intellectual unrest in the Church.

A doctor is dedicated to serving people, but he combines his sense of service with financial independence and social stability. I do not see any hope for Catholicism unless the priests re-evaluate their contribution to society and their own identity. What is a priest? Who needs priests, and what for? How can the priest best fulfill his dedication to Christ and his vocation of service to the poor? We don't need the holy priest as much as we need the wholly dedicated priest.

10. ARE SEMINARIES NECESSARY?

§ YES

Of course, seminaries are necessary. These are schools for the formation and education of priests. They are vital to the future of the Church. It is sad that even they are being saturated with false ideas on religion. When the seminarians in Brighton, Massachusetts, picketed the cardinal they violated the canons of normal decency. Recently, in another seminary, an entire group walked out after a dispute with the bishop. Yet another seminary experienced a food strike and a pray-in. This kind of individual does not belong in a seminary.

Seminarians should be trained in obedience and especially prepared to put up with difficulties and privations later on. Hence the seminary should be strong on discipline and mortification. The seminarian should be schooled in the importance of prayer in his personal life.

I object to those seminaries that allow students to date and go to dances. This is asking for trouble. Young celibates are experiencing difficulties with sex as it is. There's no point in compounding their temptations and making celibacy such a major issue with them. The reading material of the seminarian should be carefully watched, so that at his young and impressionable age he is not exposed to the half-cocked ideas that are circulating in the secular and religious press.

The Church's future is bound up with the proper training and education of its future priests. As Pius XII once said, there can be no greater and more elevated task than that of educating good priests. That is the greatest single need of the Church today— good, holy priests. If the seminary can't assure our supply for the future, who can?

❋ NO

The purpose of seminaries has long since passed. The Church needs men of vision, men who are resourceful, who are capable of assuming leadership. The present seminary system creates little boys, puts a collar and chasuble on them, and expects them to survive in our agitated and agonizing world.

Many priests today decry the training they received in the seminary. They call it unrealistic and insular, and some look back on it in anger. Many are going through an arrested adolescence and insecurity. Did they make the proper choice? Did they know what it was all about? Did they really give up their option for marriage? Do they want to be priests forever or only for a specified term? So much anxiety and so much chaos exist in the priesthood today. Certainly, the loss of priests is at a record high. In Holland almost ten percent are married. It has been predicted that in the next five years almost ten thousand priests will leave the priesthood in America.

The seminary must give up its outdated methods of training. The seminary must move to the university campus and out to the marketplace. Seminarians must be forced to manifest maturity prior to ordination. The canons for admitting a person to the priesthood should be changed. Too many milk-faced boys are coming off the seminary assembly line, boys who are rated on their ability to agree with their superiors and to follow childish rules. Turn the seminarians loose into the world, demand that they prove themselves leaders, and you will be surprised at the caliber of priest who takes his place next to you in the struggle of life. Religion will become manly and meaningful.

VIII

DEVOTIONS
AND
INVOLVEMENT

IN THE DEVOTIONAL life of the Church we can see how Catholicism is lived at the grass roots. It shows where the beliefs and the theology of the Christian faith have led us.

The devotional life of the Church has many facets. For example, we worship Christ in various ways: as the Sacred Heart, the Holy Child, the Suffering Servant on the Cross, and as he appeared to various individuals. After our central devotion to Christ, we place tremendous trust and love in the role of Mary, Mother of Christ. As the Mother of Christ, our brother, she is our mother too. If we are her humble children, she will bring us to Christ in the most perfect way. Mary is even more easily approached than Christ because, not being divine, she is more like us. We can thus get near Christ, the God-man, by asking Mary to be our guide. Her intercession is an example of God's concern for us and our inability to reach him under our own steam.

Below Mary there is a whole heavenly army to help us in our weakness. These are the saints. They have lived on earth, and they came through like knights in shining armor. Because of their perfect love for God, they have been set up by the Church as models for us to follow. They have shown by miracles either before or after their death that they had God on their side while they were on earth. What is good about the saints is that we can choose the ones we like best and emulate them as we travel on our road to self-perfection.

Of course, there is still room for our own personal contribution to our perfection. We express this contribution in prayer, which is our way of talking to God, Christ, Mary, and the saints. Even though it might often seem as if we are talking to ourselves in an empty room, we must never ask, as did Cool Hand Luke, "Are you there, Old Man? Are you there?" God is there, Mary is there, the saints are there. We've just got to keep on praying.

But we can't be perfect all the time. We're bound to doubt and make mistakes. Our devotional life provides an answer for this, too: confession. In the confessional we are alone with God (through the instrumentality of the priest). We confess our sins, and our guilt is removed. We are ready and able to start again on our arduous pilgrimage to paradise.

Our whole devotional life is aimed at personal union with God. It is geared toward self-perfection, and the method used is introspection. The basic theory of devotion is that if you perfect yourself, the world will become a better place.

Until recently, devotional life was extremely personal, and the lay person saw little need to take a leading role in his Church. But today many people are claiming that they are the Church as much as the priests are. Laymen now see their role as one that must converge with, not separate from, that of the priests. They are beginning to realize that being a Catholic is more than mere attendance at Church functions, that they must become involved.

The Church's devotional life and the role of the lay person leave many unanswered questions. Do traditional beliefs correspond to the reality of our everyday life? Do they advance the idea that a Catholic's major responsibility as a follower of Christ is to assist other people? Do they really help the Catholic become a better person? Do they leave him open enough to question their value by pondering the following questions?

1. DO YOU LIKE THE NEW LITURGY?

§ YES

I was quite disturbed when the reforms were introduced all at once. After all, I spent most of my life listening to the Church talk about the beauty of the liturgy in Latin, and how everyone in the world heard the same words in the Mass. So it was upsetting to find everything suddenly changed. But I'm getting used to it, and it's at least as good as the old way was. I enjoy hearing the prayers of the Mass recited in my own language. Yes, the liturgy seems to belong more to the people now, and after some reflection I feel that that is how it should be.

The changes in the liturgy are coming along rather quickly, but one must be open to change, so the Church tells us, and I am willing to accept that. I hope, though, that most of the changes have taken place, because I do think that we can go too far. While

I had all the respect in the world for Pope John, he was, I think, stepping on dangerous ground when he started changing the words of the Canon. Some things must remain sacred. How could we have the Consecration if we change its words?

But it is unlikely that the Church will make such a big mistake. All in all, I think that the renewal in the liturgy is very good. It fills me with great joy to see the many people who are able to join together in worship of God. And what better way to do it than at the celebration of the Eucharist when Christ our brother comes to help us praise God! I hope that interest in the liturgy grows, and that we may bring the world closer to God through this great work.

✳ NO

The renewal in the liturgy is said to be a sign of the renewal of the whole Church. Because we can pray together in our own language at Mass, we are told, we will more readily start praying side by side with people of all races and economic backgrounds. Because we can join with the priest in singing the hymns at Mass, the pastor will let us have a greater say in the running of the parish. Because we show ourselves to be the people of God at Mass, the Church will become less of an institution and more the living body of Christ. All this is nonsense. In so many instances the liturgy renewal has become a substitute for truly beneficial action.

I don't mean to knock the value of the liturgy. If it really were liturgy, if it really were the work of the people (that's what liturgy means), it would be the most important of all Catholic acts. But the renewal is a farce. We have put new wine in old wineskins, and the wine has already turned sour. We have only modernized our liturgy, simply translated it from one language to another. We have not re-created it. We have not rescued it from the frozen forms in which it has been encrusted for so many centuries. And so, when we go to Mass, we freeze also.

"The Church giveth and the Church taketh away; blessed be the name of the Church." I'm not about to accept that attitude. I've had enough of phony piety and phony worship. I can understand why some people—priests and laymen—are seeking their own forms of worship, leaving the Church behind. I love God, I love Christ, I love his Church. But I fear that the Church that claims to be Christ's Church is being abandoned by the *real* followers of Christ.

2. IS SELF-PERFECTION OUR CATHOLIC GOAL?

§ YES

Self-perfection is in our best interest and the best interest of everyone. Self-perfection means doing what Christ told us to do. Throughout his life he constantly spoke of the perfect man: humble in spirit, interested first of all in the kingdom of God, not of this world, dependent on the providence of God—even the hairs of his head are numbered. Christ pictured this man in great detail and we can help everyone by imitating this model. I am only one person. My destiny depends on God's grace and my free will. Unless I concentrate on the use of my free will, I might lose salvation by default. After all, even if I spend all my time trying to save other people, they will have to make the final decision. So why don't I just set an example for them and let them come to it on their own?

Besides, too often the apostolate turns into nothing more than social work. How many people have started with the best of intentions to help other people, only to lose the precious gift of faith themselves! It's better to look after the beam in my own eye, lest I ignore it as I try to get the splinter out of someone else's.

❄ NO

Our whole life will be judged on our efforts to help other people. I'm more interested in what Christ did than in what he said. I'm not implying that what Christ did is opposed to what he said. Rather, his actions were a demonstration of what he meant when he spoke. He cured the sick, he went without everything for the sake of his people, he had no place to lay his head. He gave up even his life so that men might know the truth and the truth might make them free.

It is in this very work that we are saved. But, overextended, the quest for perfection can become meaningless. Aiming only for perfection can be a sort of spiritual narcissism. The people who do that are selfish in the most insidious way. They think that they would be happy in heaven even if they were the only ones there. They think that Christianity was founded simply to make them happy. I believe that we are Christians in order to get to know one another and to make other people happy. Pretty altruistic perhaps, pretty idealistic maybe, but these are the facts. Christianity is not a selfish religion.

Christ said, "Be perfect as your heavenly Father is perfect." And I recall that God gave us his dearly beloved Son to help us out. St. Paul said, "Be imitators of me as I am of Christ." And I recall that Christ gave up his life to help us. It makes you wonder a little, doesn't it?

3. IS PRAYER REAL?

§ YES

Prayer is talking with God. It's not a dialogue because in a dialogue both people have an opportunity to give, and, of course, we can't give God anything. But prayer is our way of satisfying our need to thank God for what he has done, to praise him for his greatness, to apologize for having sinned against him, or to ask him for some favor. God wants this, he expects it, but, of course, since he is God, none of it affects him. He can't be moved by prayer, since he can't be changed, but we must pray so to fulfill our need to communicate with him.

It is a beautiful picture to see man, who is lowly, humble, in need of help, on his knees before an all-powerful yet loving God. If only more men could be seen in this position, the world would have a much brighter future.

✳ NO

It seems to me that much of prayer is superstition. People walk into a room—an empty room, for usually they like best to pray alone—and start talking either aloud or quietly. They say this is prayer: the words, the eyes closed or turned upward, the inclination of the heart. They are talking to God wherever he is, in the heart or in heaven or in the air.

If you criticize prayer, you are a godless man, a sinner. But I seem to remember a man once saying: When you pray, don't multiply words. The spirit is within you. The spirit is part of you.

Prayer is reflecting on the spirit that is in you. Prayer is working with the spirit that is in you. Prayer is communicating with the spirit that is in others. Prayer is sharing this spirit in you with others. Prayer is the contribution you make to the work of the spirit. Prayer is being yourself in the presence of the spirit. Prayer is being proud of yourself and your union with the spirit. Prayer is being with God.

4. ISN'T THE CONFESSIONAL REALLY JUST INSTANT PSYCHIATRY?

§ NO

People who ask this kind of question forget what they are talking about. Confession is part of the sacrament of penance, and as a sacrament it is a special sign of Christ's presence. A sacrament actually makes present what it is signifying. This is an awesome fact. Whenever we partake of a sacrament, we are in the actual presence of Christ, the sacramental presence of Christ.

So we meet Christ in a special way when we go to confession. The priest is speaking the very words of Christ, and we are therefore receiving divine advice. But, more important, we are receiving the forgiveness of Christ. We are sinners, there is no way we can deny it. We must rely on Christ's help. When we sin, we know that we can run to him and beg his pardon, and we can be sure that we will receive it, because he promised that his representatives would have his power to forgive. Without this sacrament, we would have to make a perfect Act of Contrition before we could be even a little sure that God would forgive us. While we should always try to make a perfect Act of Contrition, we can't always do it, and so an imperfect Act will merit forgiveness for us in the confessional. The confessional is no trick, no joke. It is the encounter of a sinner who has repented and a God who lovingly takes him back to his bosom.

§ YES

One of the most important aspects of psychiatric treatment is to release the tremendous guilt that lies in the heart of the patient. Once this guilt is released, the person can get to know himself better. I think that the confessional takes care of the first part of this treatment, the release of guilt. The typical Catholic has a lot to be guilty about; in fact, he begins to worry if he is feeling too happy. "No cross, what a cross," the saying goes. In my eyes much of this guilt is irrational.

The typical Catholic has been taught to be guilty about his "sinful" actions. To protect him from going insane with guilt, the Church has advanced the idea of the confessional. Who has not felt the tremendous wave of relief surging through one's body and soul after a good confession? "Go and sin no more," the priest says, and you leave the box with an optimism and joy that cannot be suppressed—until you do something that will make you feel obliged to enter that box again.

The confessional is an insidious weapon of slavery. It enslaves us to the Church, to whom we are eternally grateful for having deigned to forgive us, and separates us from the world and our fellow men, who are the ones who are really hurt by our sins. It enslaves us to introspection, to guilt, to regret. It enslaves us to a selfish, immature approach to God, worlds apart from the real religious life of active concern for the needs of others. The confessional keeps us away from this real world.

5. IS DEVOTION TO MARY UN-CHRISTIAN?

§ NO

Mary is the Mother of God. God waited for centuries to find the perfect woman to be the mother of his Son. Christ let her be with him for his whole life. She is the model of submission to God's will, she is without sin, she is the foremost example of service in God's army.

The Church has made devotion to Mary an important part of its life. Liturgical feasts, important shrines, elaborate prayers, all bespeak the great joy the Church finds in praising Mary.

One of the most saddening aberrations of the renewal is that many people are trying to "put Mary in her place," as they say. This attempt is a sign of what's wrong with the renewal in general: People want to break away from their dependence on God and the Church. Devotion to Mary is the best way to remain faithful to God. Christ was proud to be Mary's child. What can be more beautiful than to be able to sit at Mary's feet as a loving child and learn the tremendous mysteries of God's love for us? Who better than Mary, the perfect model of obedience, can show us how we should obey the authority of the Church? Who better than Mary, who was a perfect virgin all her life, can show us how to be beautifully pure? A child of Mary is a child of God!

❋ YES

The devotion to Mary as it has been practiced in the Church is un-Christian. I don't mean that we want to destroy Mary or insult her. She was a great woman, dedicated and loving when facing life, courageous when facing her Son's death. I honor Mary. I honor many of the great women of this century too. I also honor my own mother. But I am an adult, and I am my own man. I serve Christ willingly, but as I mentioned, I do it as I am—a man. Christ himself told Mary where her place was. He had to be about his Father's business.

This is not being cold or hard. I will love Mary, but I will not be her child who can do nothing on his own. I will not go to her as my queen who will take my rotten apple to the king. She is an inspiration for me because of her exemplary life. Now I must be allowed to follow Christ in my own way.

Many people may be upset by these thoughts. Devotion to Mary is very close to the heart of many Catholics. But what is so Catholic about being a humble child clinging for dear life to the hand of his mother? The hippies want to become like children, and we criticize them for escaping reality. Yet those of us who want to be free from childlike slavery to Mary are condemned for being rebellious, for being "freethinkers." Why don't you wait for some results from this thinking before you start criticizing?

6. SHOULD THE LAYMAN BE MORE THAN A MERE OBSERVER?

§ NO

The layman should keep his place in his church and not get in the way of the priests. After all, what are priests for if laymen are to be found crawling all over the sacristy and the sanctuary? I can't stand to see the layman as a lector, reading an epistle. This is not his place. His place is in the pews. What gives a layman the right to get up and take over the liturgy service? What gives him the right to preach to his fellow man? He is not a priest. Although in general I like the new liturgy, sometimes I think I got more out of the Mass when it was in Latin than I do now when some of these amateurs get up and start mumbling the prayers and giving orders to kneel and to stand.

I have heard that some priests are afraid that in the United States the heresy of trusteeism is returning again. This was bad enough in its time, when the people refused to accept their appointed pastors and even tried to run the parishes by themselves. The Church went through a terrible time just trying to keep order.

Many lay people criticize the priests and think they could

do a better job. But they don't have the training and the spiritual power to direct and protect the faithful. Many of these laymen who give priests and bishops such a hard time are ex-seminarians who dropped out of training for the priesthood, or were asked to leave for sexual reasons. Now they think they can have their revenge on the Church by spreading anticlerical ideas and giving the local priests a black eye.

I know one ex-seminarian who never goes to church on Sunday. He complains about the way priests spend money, about the food they eat and the cars they drive. To hear this man talk you would think that priests do nothing all day, and work only on weekends. He says that priests drink a lot, and take long vacations and long naps. Most of the lay people see through this dropout from the priesthood. One lady asked him candidly why he left the seminary if the priesthood was such a soft racket. He couldn't answer that one.

We need the priests who work so hard. I think, to run the Church, today especially, priests need special training and special help from God. Priests pray all day, and work at their vocation. The layman is concerned with his own family and with his own problems. He needs help from the priest. The layman should be happy to be in a church that has a full-time staff of devoted priests ready to serve him at a moment's notice.

✳ YES

Most priests would like to keep the layman out of their hair. That way they can run the parish the way they want, without interference. They can have their own budget and can take their own sweet time in doing things.

The layman is the Church, and the layman is as much a Catholic as the priest. I know many laymen who are more intelligent, more human, and more spiritual than many priests. Some of the sermons I have heard in my parish would bore a five-year-old. Priests in general think the layman is a moron and that he should be seen and not heard. But the layman is the one who pays the bills for the parish. The layman is the one who must scrimp and save and do without to fill his monthly collection envelope. The layman is the one who must bear the brunt of the criticism against the Church. There is an old Catholic proverb, "The voice of the people is the voice of God." In the consensus of a parish you can usually strike the real voice and direction of the Church.

One problem we are facing is that our parish priests are mainly administrators. The parishes are too large. The priests have a rough time taking care of the material aspects of the parish, since the parish is like a big business, what with a school, convent, church, and rectory. All this demands time for proper administration. Little wonder that priests go out to the golf course and fancy restaurants just to get away from it all and catch their breath. The parish of tomorrow should have a board of trustees to look after these material concerns. Thus the priest would be free to follow his spiritual mission, for which he has been trained. He would have time for his priestly duties, whatever they might be in these changing times.

The diocese also needs to take the layman more seriously. I have never met my bishop. I seldom meet my pastor. I seldom see the priests on a human basis. I find that since Vatican II I resent being treated like a dollar sign in the parish ledgers.

7. HAS THE CHURCH DONE ITS DUTY TOWARD BLACK PEOPLE?

§ YES

I know that the Catholic Church today is coming under heavy fire, even from black priests, as being a white, racist church. I know that many black people look on the Church in resentment and even hate. Yet I know that there are two orders in the United States that have taken good care of the black people. The Josephite Fathers especially are the friends of the black man, and they have been good and devoted friends. White people in the North have given this group of dedicated men the money and materials necessary to carry out their work.

I think that the Church has been kind to the black man. But

the Church hasn't ever gone to the defense of any one race, has it? I mean, the Italians, the Poles, and even the Irish were a persecuted and scorned people in the United States as late as twenty-five years ago. Though the Church admirably cared for these people, it never helped one group to the exclusion of others. The Church has always been all things to all men. It has especially helped those who were willing to help themselves.

The Catholic Church has never refused admittance to a person because of his color. It has sent missionaries to Africa, many of whom died in the service of black people. The Catholic Church has really tried to help black people, but so many of them have not wanted to help themselves.

✷ NO

The Catholic Church has failed black people miserably. It does not do any good to cite instances of individual priests and nuns aiding black people. One has to look at the philosophy and social doctrine of the Catholic Church and how it has been fulfilled in a leadership role. This is the nub of the whole problem. Priests and nuns may have gone to the aid of the Negro people, and the bishops in 1956 or thereabouts condemned racism and all it implies. Yet today the race problem has blown up in the Church's face.

The nuns who went on picket lines and marched in civil-rights demonstrations have had to suffer at the hands of the Church. Many of them have since left their orders, or are silenced in some remote convent. Father Groppi in Milwaukee is a good example of a priest who has tried to push the Church into a realistic posture on civil rights. But what support did he receive from the Church?

Catholics in general have not been very Christian to their black brothers. I heard many priests make fun of Martin Luther King while he was alive, and even ridicule his work among the poor. Then when Dr. King was assassinated, these same priests began to realize how much more dynamic and Christian was his ministry in comparison to theirs. I don't think that the Catholic Church could ever produce a priest of Dr. King's stature and influence, simply because it has never allowed its priests the freedom and support necessary to lead black people out of bondage.

A simple comparison between Dr. King's brand of Christianity and the one practiced by the majority of Catholics is sufficient to point up the weaknesses of the Catholic Church in the field of race relations. The Catholic Church has shown no leadership. It has failed to provide its membership with direction. It has been subservient to the white power structure. And it has been especially beholden to the financial power of the white race, aware that contributions would diminish if it spoke out strongly on the delicate question of race. The Catholic Church betrayed its heritage and abandoned its principles for money. It tolerated separate churches, separate schools, and separate communion rails for too long. The Church may very well have sounded its own death knell when it turned from the black people and chose to serve affluent whites, keeping silence rather than letting the real message of Christianity ring out.

8. SHOULD THE CHURCH PROMOTE PACIFISM?

§ NO

There is such a thing as a just war. There is such a thing as self-defense. We are all against killing just for the sake of killing. But in a just war there is an unjust aggressor. If we say that Americans should not be fighting in Vietnam, for instance, then we are saying that we should simply turn the other cheek and let any enemy run riot over our homes and our loved ones. This is not Christianity. Christ said that he came not to bring peace, but the sword; that he came to set brother against brother, and so on. If it advocated pacifism, the Church would be rejecting the example of Christ and leaving itself open to eventual extinction. We must fight for what is right.

Cardinal Spellman won the hearts of many people because he cared about our fighting forces. He visited them every year and saw the atrocities committed by the enemy against helpless peoples and American soldiers. He called on Americans to be patriotic and loyal to their President. He said, "My country, right or wrong." I believe in this. And I think the Church had better get this message across to the bearded beatniks and peaceniks. Freedom is not easy to preserve. It is precious. Everyone who enjoys it should be willing to die for it. Only with loyal and patriotic citizens can a nation hope to survive.

❋ YES

For most of its past, the Catholic Church has not been a peace-loving organization. The Church has survived to this date despite its ancient, creaking philosophy and theology simply because it has been able to crush its enemies. The holy wars of the Crusades and the Inquisition are evidence that the Church has used war to protect its own interests. Pius XII did not condemn the Nazis as he should have because he hoped that the Nazis would engage the communists in battle and an atheistic enemy would be routed. He looked the other way when the gas ovens of Dachau and Auschwitz were in full swing. The Catholic Church through history has been guilty of expediency and pragmatism. Its philosophy has been that the ends justify the means, especially in regard to war. Thus in its role as war advocate, the Catholic Church has blurred the image of the Prince of Peace. He preached love and charity and justice. He scolded Peter for drawing a sword to protect him in the garden of Gethsemane. "He who takes the sword shall perish by the sword," Christ said.

The Catholic Church should encourage pacifism simply because the world has suffered too much from too many wars. "There's enough death and pain, without adding to the game," goes the song. This is so true. A Church that advocates war is not the Church that Christ founded.

Pope Paul came to the United Nations and pleaded for an end to all wars. Do you realize that if we don't stamp out wars, we will one day be wiped out? Men have to learn to respect one another, and to uphold the other's right to dissent. Solutions to disagreement are not to be found in killing the opposition, but in patient discussion at the negotiating table. This is what Pope

John XXIII advocated in his encyclicals. I don't see the communists of today as the big bad wolves of five years ago. They are human beings, and they want to live. They have as much to lose as the free world does in the event of total global war. Pacifism means using truly Christian means to settle differences, and ultimately to achieve a brotherhood among men. The Catholic Church had better advocate this, lest the stale odor of a militant patriotism offend the Creator.

9. SHOULD THE CHURCH FIGHT AGAINST THE USE OF MARIJUANA?

§   YES

Marijuana, or "pot," is a narcotic, a drug, and as such its use is illegal. A lot of kids today are using pot. They are looking for kicks and trying to expand their consciousness. This is an artificial device, for it tampers with the laws of nature. Because pot is against the law of man and the law of nature, its use should be prohibited. The fact that so many kids smoke pot, and so many good people use it once in a while, does not make it right. This "mob rule" tactic bespeaks a loss of logic and sound objectivity.

The youth of today have everything they want and need. They have cars, spending money, college educations, and the best of everything. And still they are not satisfied. They have to drop out of society. They poke all sorts of accusations at the establishment. I know that one of the basic reasons behind the use of pot is that it is an escape from reality. What are they running from? Responsibility. Kids want to have, but they don't want to work. They think that everything is due them and that their families should support their experimentation and rebellion. The kids' use of pot is a rejection of our society. They have one hell of a nerve. We give them the world, and they spit in our faces and puff on a weed.

The responsibility of our young people should be to help those who are less fortunate than themselves. The past decade has seen soaring achievements. We adults must have done something right. We are not the only ones responsible for the mess the world is in. But even if we were, the kids are not helping things when they run away from it. Pot is a flight from reality.

✳ NO

Pot is not harmful. Medical science has shown that it is a light depressant and that it is not habit-forming. It does not necessarily lead to the use of hard drugs. Pot is a good relaxant, and its effects are far less deleterious than alcohol. I know medical students who use pot prior to exam time. They claim it helps relax them. It also helps them concentrate on their studies. They say it's like a form of self-hypnosis that expands the consciousness and helps impress things on the mind.

Pot is outlawed in the United States, but I don't know why. There have been dangerous drugs outlawed previously, but only after long scientific investigations. Until recently no one had done any worthwhile research on pot and its medical implications. And the more research that is done, the less harmful pot seems to be. Cigarette smoking is dangerous to health, but because of the powerful tobacco lobby in Congress the only "protection" we have is a silly label on the cigarette package.

We should be asking ourselves *why* kids turn to pot. Therein lies the mammoth embarrassment. Kids get more out of a stick of grass than they do out of a religious service. They find the Catholic liturgy boring and useless. They would rather sit down at a pot party and share their thoughts with others of the same mind. Pot's use is more a rejection of religion and society than anything else. The kids reject society because of its sheer hypocrisy. Parents blast their kids for using pot, but they themselves go on alcoholic benders. Parents force their kids to go to church, but they themselves look on religion as merely a social obligation. Kids see their parents cheating, cursing, fighting, gossiping, and turn thumbs down on any religion or value system that explains away such conduct.

Instead of condemning the young and making pot a big issue, we should try to find out the reasons behind this generation's rejection of society. If there is any validity to the reasons, we had better do something about it quickly. Because the kids are not going to wait for us. As Bob Dylan puts it, "You'd better start moving or sink like a stone, for the times they are a-changing."

10. DO YOU THINK THAT THE CHURCH HAS LOST THE TEEN-AGER?

§ NO

I think the teen-ager has lost the Church. The Church is eternal and will survive. The gates of hell shall not prevail against it. Kids need the Church, and they cannot last without the saving balm of the Church's aid. The Church is Jesus Christ, now, yesterday, and forever. Christ loved the young, and he turns his heart toward them in pity and sadness. But he will not be mocked, and he will not be insulted. If the kids don't want the Church, then they will in fact go to hell.

I wouldn't mind if the Church was not trying to woo the teen-ager, but the parishes sponsor dances, picnics, teen-age Masses, and in some places even folk Masses. The kids are still not happy. Perhaps they want to make God over to their own image and likeness. Priests spend hours trying to teach the young people in religion classes, and the kids make fun of the priests and even criticize the teachings of the Church. What the teen-ager today needs is a pat on the back, often enough and low enough. I know a priest who said that the teen-ager is rebellious and scornful of the Church now but that when he is older or is sick he'll change his tune. Just let teen-agers look into the fires of hell and their epithets of rage will turn into cries of fear.

Our kids today are spoiled, and I hope that the Church doesn't back down on its sacred trust and try to compromise with them. Kids do not know it all, no matter what they think. The Church has been around longer than any of us, and it knows how to weather any storm. I weep not for the Church, but for the young people. They have never had it so good, nice schools, lots of money, the best of everything. If they can't give one hour a week to serious worship and an hour to catechism, then they don't deserve any sympathy. The Church should not relax its discipline to suit the fitful moods of adolescents.

✳ YES

The Church has lost the teen-ager. Kids don't pay any attention to the Church. Even those in Catholic schools are merely putting up with the Church until they graduate. This is a tragedy, since the Church could do so much to help them. But the Church is too steeped in Tradition and ancient rites to let the message of Christ show through. And this ancient rust is what makes young people bitter.

The Church has abdicated its role in the lives of the young. And who has taken up this role but the commercial world? The record industry especially is growing fat on the young, and at the same time is filling their minds with new values and new mores. And the kids are listening, because the record industry is on their wave length. The kids look on the Church as an old God-fogey. The nuns and priests have nothing to say but "Don't do this, don't do that." The kids say "Why not?" And the same answer comes through—because it is evil. Kids try to see the world as shining and wonderful and beautiful. Their religion tells them it is insidious and lethal. The kids say it isn't so. They turn their backs on the horror tales of the Catholic religion.

The rebellion of the young against organized religion should be carefully attended to, because the young are the adults of tomorrow. Only God can tell what a terrible explosion will rack the Catholic Church if the young people continue to reject it. Where will you and I be then? The Church should get out among the young, learn their language and their lore, and adapt itself to their needs and their yearnings. Christ became a man to win over men. There is no reason to believe that he would not do this again in order to capture the idealism and imagination of youth today. Youth is civilization's rainbow. And there is no rainbow glow over the Catholic Church today. Who will bear the responsibility for tomorrow's storm?

IX

NUNS,
RELIGIOUS
LIFE,
AND
CATHOLIC
SCHOOLS

Nuns have always been the darlings of the Catholic Church. Pictures regularly appear in the secular and religious press showing the good sisters skiing, playing baseball, swimming, and enjoying other innocent things that people seem to find extremely amusing when nuns do them. For nuns are supposed to be sweet and angelic, something out of the Hollywood mind, as in the movie *Going My Way*. Of course, once in a while, another side of convent life emerges when someone like Monica Baldwin, who wrote *I Leapt over the Wall*, tells all the dark and mysterious secrets of the cloister.

Nuns only began to be taken seriously by the general public when pictures of them on picket lines, and especially in the Selma march, made the front pages all over the nation. Many people seemed hurt at seeing the nuns in places where nuns are not supposed to be. After all, they felt, nuns do not have minds of their own but must have their activities sanctioned by the reverend mother or the bishop. How dare anyone imagine that nuns could be interested in civil rights or peace demonstrations!

Now nuns are really making news. They are changing their habits, their religious habits as well. Sister Corita, the famous artist, and now ex-nun, is photographed wearing miniskirts and drinking cocktails. Nuns are leaving the convent in droves. Many nuns are wearing lay clothes and influencing thought and policy not only in the Church, but also in the secular world.

Most people identify nuns with hospitals and schools. Nuns run some of the largest hospitals in the nation, and therefore many people come into close contact with them. They are seen as angels of mercy (although most of them are involved in the administrative end of hospital work or in a supervisory capacity). It is the same in schools. Parents are used to having their children come home and mouth parrot-like whatever sister told them in school. "But Sister said!" is a common rejoinder in many homes.

Without the nuns the Catholic Church would long since have faded away. In the past the nuns were content to work in humble seclusion out of the public eye. But such is no longer the case.

How do you feel about the emerging and articulate nun of the twentieth century? Do you think that nuns are going too far, especially in their radical departures from the traditional forms of religious life?

How do you feel about Catholic schools? Do you think the Catholic school system is an unnecessary financial burden on the average lay person? Do you think that the curriculum is vastly inferior, as some critics maintain? Do you think that Catholic schools should be phased out? In this chapter we will consider some thoughts on the sisterhood, the religious life, and Catholic schools.

1. DO YOU AGREE WITH THE CHANGES IN NUNS' ATTITUDES?

§   NO

I think that many nuns are losing the respect and admiration of the general public by their behavior. They are also arousing the wrath of many sincere people. Nuns belong in their convents. Why did they enter if they are going to spend so much time getting into things that do not concern them? It is difficult to recognize a nun today, with all the changes in the religious habit. Now nuns are showing off their legs, and even getting fancy hairdos. That a nun should dress like an ordinary lay person is incomprehensible.

We used to be proud to see a nun in public, in her holy habit. She was a sign of the presence of the Church. People respected her and looked up to her. She was a sign of virginity and purity, and she did not seem to be an ordinary woman. Now I see men eyeing nuns as though they were available women. If a nun is attacked, I don't think I would feel sorry for her. In fleeing the religious habit, she is asking for trouble.

The children in school do not speak respectfully of the sisters any more. They have such weird ideas on freedom and obedience, they wear lipstick and makeup and even nail polish. They have lost their sense of other-worldliness. We have lost a great thing in destroying the traditional image of the nun.

✳ *YES*

In general, the nuns are making significant strides. Of course, I cannot see all the to-do about the habit. For me it is quite simple. The habit is simply a throwback to past centuries, and besides being cumbersome and awkward, it is just plain ugly. I would rather see the nuns in lay clothes. There again, I think we get hung up on incidentals. But I am happy to see the nuns getting out with the lay people. If in the past nuns were treated like children and patronized by priests and laity alike, it is because they asked for it. They put their holy rule and reverend mother above everything else, and as a result no one in the real world took them seriously. Now that the nuns are becoming involved with people, you can speak to a nun after eight o'clock in the evening and identify with her as a person and not as an awesome vestal virgin. This augurs great promise for the Church. Nuns for so many years seemed to thrive on strict discipline; they were mechanical in their actions and in their manner of speech. Everything about them seemed dollish and artificial. Any change in this kind of thing is progress. The nuns are a force that the Church has never fully utilized. Now with the barriers down and the individual emerging, perhaps we can expect more leadership from the convents.

2. DO YOU KNOW WHAT RELIGIOUS LIFE IS?

§ *YES*

Religious life is the way of life within the Catholic Church whereby an elite few endeavor to observe the counsels of perfection laid down by Christ. "If thou wilt be perfect, go sell what thou hast and give to the poor, and thou shalt have treasure in heaven; and come, follow me" (Matthew 19:21). Although there is no mention of religious orders in the Bible, the principles that inspired their beginnings are surely shown in the life and teaching of Christ. Men and women join religious orders in answer to a divine call, and they thus pledge themselves to seek perfection, living under an approved rule that helps them to love God more perfectly and all men for the sake of God.

The religious life cannot be understood without relating it to a specific order. All religious orders are not the same, and, of course, they are not even essential to Christianity. We know that the Pope crushed the Jesuits in 1773, and even if all religious orders disappeared tomorrow the Church would still be around with all her God-given doctrine, law, and liturgy. Religious life is governed by canon law. To live the religious life we need communal living, but we also need authority and canonical approval. The religious life cannot exist without vows, those promises whereby a person dedicates his total being to Christ and swears to live in poverty, chastity, and obedience. People who take religious vows do not promise the impossible. The vows are difficult, but with the grace of God all things are possible. Religious life, then, is a promise to strive for perfection, and religious live a communal life so that each can support the other in this difficult vocation.

Civilization owes the religious orders a debt that it can never repay. The medieval monks were the true fathers of agriculture, reclaiming millions of acres of unfertile land in every country of Europe. They copied thousands of manuscripts of the Bible, founded many famous schools, and helped the poor, the sick, the prisoners, and even the lepers. It was the monks who brought the faith to Ireland and Germany, and the vast majority of the world owes its knowledge of the Gospel to these faithful adherents of the religious life. The religious life is a struggle for perfection, and the pages of history glow with shining examples of men and women who upheld their vows despite the hardships and difficulties on the road to perfection.

Today, we do not see too much of this and, as a consequence, the concept of religious life has become dim and unattractive. Life is a challenge, and the laity should be grateful to have the spiritual guidance of men who have renounced the pleasures of the world in order to find complete happiness in Jesus Christ.

❋ NO

I know that religious life is not the religious order. But I do not know what religious life is, and I am not unhappy about it. Life is supposed to be an unknown quantity anyhow. Life is to be lived, and no one can know what the future holds. Religious life has been frozen into a particular form for so long that to get it to move with the currents of life in general is proving an insuperable task. If we are going to restore the concept of religious life as a response to the call of Christ, we must return to the sources of Christian life.

Religious orders must return to the original spirit of their founders, and they must adapt to the changing pace of modern times. There must be a closer rapport between the Church and the religious orders, so that the orders do not put themselves forth as holier than the Church. Vatican II suggested that the manner of living, praying, and working in religious orders be adapted to the physical and psychological circumstances of the members within the religious community. Obsolete laws must be suppressed; constitutions, customs, books, and prayers must be updated. Poverty especially must be practiced in new forms, that is, religious orders must be poor in fact as well as in spirit.

I believe that the concept of vows is an obsolete one. A religious after all is a Catholic who promises God to renew the commitment contained in baptism. Why should he be asked to go through a superfluous ritual, embodying a supposed new contract, when such a contract is not required? Religious life should not be an isolated, super-Christian way of life. We have had enough separation between religious life and Catholicism in the past. The insistence on special vows of poverty, chastity, and obedience only accentuates a specious distinction between the religious and the laity.

The religious life is following Christ, a task all Christians are committed to. Religious life should be total response, with fewer vows and more community. It is the task of the religious to be an example of Christian unity, which unity is achieved through basic respect for one another and going forth into the world to serve one's neighbor.

It is regrettable that most religious orders are bent more on preserving their own identity than on expanding the entity of Christ. In so doing, they are crushing out religious life, or at least making it difficult for authentic expressions of religious life to exist. It is only through experimentation that we will discover what religious life is. We have enough contemporary examples to prove what it is not. If the Church is in turmoil today, much blame can be laid at monastery and convent doors, those doors that have refused to open up to a world God so loved that he sent his only begotten Son to save it.

3.   IS THE PRESENT FORM OF RELIGIOUS LIFE OUTMODED?

§   NO

Religious life is an expression of the evangelical counsel, and is lived communally with others who have sworn vows of poverty, chastity, and obedience. This way of life can never be outmoded, for it is the way recommended by Christ. He did not ask all Christians to practice the vows, but challenged anyone who could do it. Religious life, then, will always be with us, so long as there are people generous and self-sacrificing enough to dedicate themselves completely to the service of Christ and the Gospel.

Today many nuns, some of whom have spent years in the convent, are giving up their vows and going back into the world. I cannot understand how nuns who have made perpetual vows can give them up. Just as marriage vows are taken forever, nuns should not be permitted to renounce their vows. We need dedicated nuns to help care for the sick and the needy. We need nuns to teach in our schools and brothers to help in the training of our young men. Who will do this if the religious life is considered obsolete? What criterion are people using when they describe the religious life as outmoded? Certainly not the Gospel or the example of Christ.

The spirit of the world has crept into the convents. In his excellent biography William Thomas Walsh shows that this occurred in St. Theresa's time and that she found the convents of her day filled with worldliness. She entered the Carmelites and reformed the order and, in so doing, reformed all of religious life. That's what's needed today: a reformation in the style of Theresa, and not a mass exodus.

✻ YES

You have to make a distinction. Religious life is one thing and the way religious life is lived is another. It's simply the difference between an ideal and the practical expression of that ideal. Religious life is something we'll always need. This is the generosity of the Christian life and the expression of a heart on fire with love of God and man.

Where we have difficulty is in the present forms of religious life, with the huge structures, the vast financial empires, and the lack of creative response to genuine need in the world. The religious should be leaders, they should be sources of inspiration to the universal Church. What many priests and nuns are saying as they leave the religious life is not "I don't want to be a religious," but rather, "I can't be a religious in this system." Present religious societies are self-centered and seek to preserve their own systems at the expense of the person. When the large religious orders see their members as individuals and allow them to experiment with new forms of religious life, the orders may phase themselves out, but in the long run they will be doing a service to the Church and to the Gospel.

What we need today are small, dynamic groups of men and women who are equipped to meet the challenges of the modern world and not simply content with canonizing hoary traditions. Let's support the ex-nun and ex-priest, and try to find ways of helping them regain their identity and usefulness. There is a great potential hidden in the convents of our land. It will take nothing short of a St. Bernard or a Vincent de Paul to capitalize on the basic inspiration of religious life and make it work in the twentieth

century. Vatican II has signaled "Go." Religious societies have to
do the rest.

4. IS IT NECESSARY TO CHANGE THE NATURE OF VOCATIONS TO SOLVE THE VOCATION CRISIS?

§ NO

Four cardinals in Rome recently said that there is a genuine
crisis in recruiting people and that many mission countries are not
getting enough priests and nuns to staff their institutions. Catholic
schools throughout the country are begging for more teaching
nuns. Some hospitals are turning over their facilities to lay people
because nuns are not available. Many young people are not interested in the religious life, and vocations are falling off.

What we have here is a breakdown in the proper understanding of what a nun or a priest is and what he or she is supposed
to do. If the nuns and the priests and the brothers were happy
in their jobs and doing what they pledged themselves to do, the
Church wouldn't be having such trouble getting young people
interested in the religious life. This I think is the reason for the
problem. So many nuns are acting out of character that it is no
wonder kids are confused. Then too, so many of our young people
do not have the generosity of spirit that it takes to enter a convent or seminary. They want to have everything on their own
terms, and at the first opposition from their superior they walk
out. Many parents are discouraging their children from entering
religious life, because they are not happy with what nuns and
priests are doing. So I think we have a corrosion of the very fabric
of Church life.

Let's put the blame squarely where it belongs, and then let's
do something about the problem of miniskirted nuns and nuns
outside the walls at night. If the nuns lived their spiritual lives
properly, and spent more time in the chapel praying as they used
to do, then God would bless the various communities with voca-

tions. He is not pleased, and the people are not pleased; the young people are confused, and so vocations are down.

✳ YES

Young people are no longer interested in entering religious life. Why should they be, when all they can look forward to is a medieval form of existence in which the superior takes the place of God and the holy rule takes precedence over reason and freedom?

What are the religious doing today? There are many nuns involved in jobs that lay persons can do—and can do better. There are priests teaching algebra or English. What young person wants to enter religious life in order to do something he can do outside it? He has the Peace Corps, VISTA, and other organizations that can give him better training and do not infringe upon human dignity or the rights of the individual. Why should a young man become a Jesuit or a Dominican and endure an adolescence of fifty years or more?

The big structures are coming down, and the authorities are frantically trying to save them in the wrong way. Initiative is suppressed, experiments are tabled, and any attempt to move the religious life into the twentieth century is met with heavy-handed discipline that can only inspire rebellion. One religious order lost thirty nuns in one year, all of whom had been in the religious life for ten or fifteen years. They can't all be wrong. What about the scandal of the Immaculate Heart of Mary sisters in California? All they wanted to do was update their way of life, and they were squelched by an eighty-year-old Cardinal. And Rome supported the Cardinal. Is it any wonder that young people have second thoughts about giving their lives to a dying system?

5. ARE THERE ANY ADVANTAGES TO THE CATHOLIC SCHOOL SYSTEM?

§ YES

The Catholic school has a very important function: It provides a basic Christian education. Moreover, the contact with the Church from an early age provides the child with a foundation for his faith. He sees it lived and is close to the mainstream of orthodoxy. He gets in the habit of going to confession regularly, and the nuns see that he fulfills his Christian obligations. How often do people remember the training given them by the good nuns! How often do they look back fondly to the catechism lessons and the stories the sisters used to illustrate various points of doctrine. The discipline is good for the child, and I know many non-Catholics who will not move into a particular area unless they are sure they can get their children into a Catholic school. The children are taught genuine morality and are given a proper set of values.

The standard of education is higher in Catholic schools than in public schools. I know boys and girls who enrolled in a Catholic school and had to repeat or go back a grade because their public school did not have the high standards of the Catholic system. The nuns are dedicated, and they have the welfare of the child at heart.

The support of our Catholic school system is a double tax burden on my family, but we think that the superior training and over-all education make it more than worth the price.

❋ NO

The Catholic school system provides no real advantage over the public school system, particularly when one tries to justify the heavy financial burden it imposes on an already tax-ridden community. I think of education as the training of the whole man. I don't want to jeopardize the liberal education of my children.

I want their learning experience to be stimulating, not stunted by mediocrity.

I don't think that half the nuns in our schools are academically equipped, because so many religious communities skimp on formal education. There are few Master's degrees in the Catholic school system. Many Catholics are satisfied with having a nun with little formal education or on-the-job training teach their children a good lesson in catechism and a better understanding of a religion that comes across as largely irrelevant. I send my children to school to learn, and not to be filled with stories about angels and saints. Classrooms in Catholic schools are overcrowded, and the fact that the priest of the parish is the real boss hurts the cause of education more than anything else. Many Catholics are satisfied with substandard courses so long as they are given in gleaming new schools staffed by nuns.

Putting the child in a Catholic school often turns him sour on religion. Many people today don't bother to go to any religious worship because they were turned off by the regimentation and the heavy discipline of their youth in a Catholic school system. The children in the public schools get a better education and are offered a broader training. They are able to see religion as a way of life and not have it forced down their throats by overzealous nuns. If the public school can do the job as well, if not better, why pay to have an inferior educational system?

6. SHOULD THE CHURCH
    CONTROL EDUCATION?

§   YES

The vocation of the Church is to teach mankind the Gospel, for the Church is in charge of divine truths and is the guardian of men's morals. People feel that simply because the Church asserts its right to teach mankind that it is hostile toward other educational systems, such as the public school system, because they usurp the right given the Church by Jesus Christ. The public school system is not equipped to impart the necessary moral and religious training to our young people. The Supreme Court has driven God and the mere mention of his name from the classroom. The Church sees this terrible gap in the total training of youth, and honestly feels that since it has the promise of divine help and assistance, it must live up to its obligation.

The state has no right to hamper private initiative or set up a monopoly in education. Freedom of education is a right granted by the Constitution. Our duties to our Creator take precedence over all other duties. We may produce scholars in an atheistic environment, but we must realize that this will not develop the will and direct young people to the practice of virtue. An education that unites intellectual, moral, and religious elements is the best training for citizenship. Catholic-school graduates are generally good citizens, for they have a sense of responsibility, a respect for authority, and a considerable attitude toward the rights of others. The omission of religious instruction is a flaw in public education and can only hurt society in general. The first American schools and colleges were religious schools.

Catholics have undergone severe burdens to support their schools. They have been compelled to pay a double tax. The cost of the school system is tremendous and could never have been met were it not for the generosity of thousands of nuns, priests, and brothers who contented themselves with a paltry salary so that the Church could exercise its right to educate the total man. The Church has ever been alert that the parochial school system turn out patriotic citizens. The Church is not only faithful to its divine commission to teach all nations, but is also watchful that Catholic students love and respect the nation of their birth.

✳ NO

Vatican II made it clear that the Church has a role in education, but not the total role. All men have an inalienable right to education. The Church cannot be the source of all wisdom, and it certainly has no record to support such a claim, regardless of what the clergy say. Scientific and technological progress has been achieved despite the narrowness of the Catholic Church's educational system. The right to educate is clearly stated by Vatican II as belonging to parents. As parents have conferred life on their children, they must be acknowledged as the first and foremost educators of their children.

The Church in the past has confused education with propagandizing. Because it wanted to mold the minds of young people, the Church made it seem a mortal sin for a person to attend any school other than a Catholic one. Sophisticated Catholics long ago saw through this, and refused to surrender their children to inferior curricula and overcrowded classrooms. The first school must always be the family, whose obligation it is to create an atmosphere of love and respect for God and man.

Both God and man are important in the life of the child, and it is here that the Church has failed. Catholic schools give children an unrealistic image of God and a false impression of man and the world we live in. Catholic education is mostly polemical, in which a child is taught a strict morality that makes Catholics, especially nuns and priests, seem right and the rest of the world wrong. The propaganda that passes for Catholic education has indeed been the cause of painful experiences for many adults.

In the Catholic system sincere educators are forced to work for a subminimal wage, and their academic freedom is cruelly curbed. The heavy teaching loads given to nuns have caused many a nervous condition or a cynical approach to life.

I believe we should continue to have Catholic schools, but I hope that not only will they compete realistically with other institutions but that, moreover, the stigma of attending other than Catholic schools will disappear. We cannot insist too much on the Church's right to educate, but the days of its presumed superiority and exclusivity are long since gone.

7. WOULD YOU LIKE TO SEE MORE RELIGIOUS HOUSES IN THE SLUMS?

§ NO

It seems to me this would be a good thing if necessary, but is it? Is the risk equal to the amount of good that would be achieved? Many nuns and brothers go to work in the slums, but we cannot expect them to live there full time. The slums are a jungle, and every day we read of murders, robberies, and rapes there. Imagine what our nuns would have to go through. The Congo in recent years would be nothing compared to the terrors of the slums.

Not long ago a group of nuns who suddenly found themselves living in a deprived area had to put bars on the windows. Several times they found strange men wandering the convent corridors, terrifying the poor sisters. Their car was often damaged and the tires slashed. They pleaded for a change of residence and were told to remain in the ghetto. It wasn't until one of the nuns was almost driven out of her mind by fear that the priest in charge acquiesced and allowed them to live elsewhere.

Idealistic people often argue that religious belong in the slums, but often they do not realize the kind of a life they are foisting on them. I have heard of brothers who, after living in the slums, ended up leaving their order or becoming highly critical of the Church.

A slum is an abnormal situation, one that is brought on in large part by the unwillingness of the people there to do something for themselves. In the United States and other Western countries, with all the opportunities and vast systems of education, and all the welfare and social agencies available, it seems incredible that a person could allow himself to remain for any length of time in a ghetto. What good would it do to endanger the lives of our young religious by putting them in such an anarchistic situation? Slum people have the best social and medical help available to them, so forcing the religious to live there would not be much solace to the poor. Rather, let the religious work in the ghettos, and then have the option of returning to a convent or rectory in a respectable neighborhood.

✳ YES

The religious life is a response to need, and it must be a total response. Christ exemplified this need when he came among men and subjected himself to human infirmities. He showed himself to be the friend of the poor, and preached the gospel of love to them. Christ is the exemplar of the religious in every sense of the term. Nuns and priests vow a life of poverty, chastity, and obedience, and these vows are made on behalf of humanity. If they try to be selective about what needs they will respond to, then they abjure their commitment to the religious life.

People in the slums are disadvantaged. They are told to pull themselves up by their bootstraps, but the majority of them do not even own boots. They are rejected by society and accused of all kinds of crime. The crime rate is high in the slums, because the sense of injustice overwhelms the people. The people in the slums need Christ, the Christ who will comfort, who will calm, who knows no prejudice. Nuns and priests, as representatives of Christ and of his unifying influence, belong in the slums. This is their vocation and their life. The risks are great, but they are not insurmountable.

Why is it that when a neighborhood gets rundown and poor, the Church moves out? Isn't it because it places a premium on services and not service?

Nuns and priests are committed to serve Christ by serving the poor. They must be prepared to sacrifice and to respond with deep responsibility to the fallen and rejected masses in the ghettos. They must go out armed with faith in their vocation and in human dignity. They can shower the slum dwellers with kindness, meekness, and mercy. They can get into areas that the nine-to-five social worker just doesn't have time to reach. They must bring themselves, full persons, armed with a mission and a mandate for change. In the shadow of our cathedrals poor children, hungry children, rejected children huddle. Where is the risen Christ? they ask. Where is the love of the Christian? This is the vocation of the religious, for it is in the slums that Christ bleeds and is lonely.

I know of a letter that was written to the Pope by the Superior General of the Jesuits asking that the huge monumental seminaries be closed and that the young priests of tomorrow be trained in today's slums. A religious must let his life be dominated by the needs of others. He must confront those needs with vision and tolerance and deep generosity. Far from endangering the religious life, living in the slums could bring about a revitalization of true religious life.

8. ARE YOU IN FAVOR OF CATHOLIC HOSPITALS?

§ YES

The care of the sick has been a distinctively Catholic service down through the centuries, so it was only natural that when health care began to center in large medical institutions the Catholic Church found itself in the forefront. Now in almost every large city and small town you will find a Catholic hospital.

In Catholic hospitals patients get a little more than the ordinary care. A nun at your bedside in time of pain and suffering helps to lift your mind up to God. During the war the soldiers called the nuns "angels of mercy," and so they were. Sisters spend long hours on the hospital floor, going beyond the call of duty. They are cheerful and smiling; to them, care of the sick never degenerates into a disagreeable chore or a mere business relationship. I regret that the staff of sisters in some hospitals is so meager that the nuns cannot devote as much time to bedside care as in the past. In my city the sisters have several large hospitals, and they do excellent work with young children. They have a special talent with children, and it is really rewarding to go through the wards with a nun and see how the children's faces light up when they see her.

The Catholic Church not only has superior medical facilities, but it also serves the community in another important way: It minimizes the frequency of immoral operations. Abortions and sterilizations are kept down, because the doctors know that the nuns will not tolerate any violations of Church law. The dead also receive all the respect due them. Autopsies are performed with dignity and with sensitivity, because the nuns instill respect through the entire staff. At the moment of death the nuns make sure that a priest is present and that the family is given the consolation of knowing that their beloved died in the arms of Holy

Mother Church. Futile experimentation is not tolerated in Catholic hospitals. The care of the sick and dying is such an important vocation that the Church by the very nature of its mission cannot afford to ignore it.

Catholic hospitals give more than their share of care to charity patients, who are treated not only in the hospital, but through effective out-patient care and social agencies connected with the hospital. Let's hope that the Church always maintains its proper role in the care of the sick.

❋ NO

I am not in favor of any form of segregation, including separate hospitals for Catholics. The Catholic hospital is an outgrowth of our former siege mentality. We had to put Catholics in special hospitals because we were afraid that this was the only way that our faithful would be sure of expert care and attention.

The Church has spent millions of dollars setting up large, separate facilities. Now they are faced with the very real problem of staffing these institutions, for there are so few young nuns emerging from our convents. Today, when medical care is so specialized and highly efficient, the distinctly Catholic unit has become an anachronism. I know of one order of nursing nuns that sends its nuns into the local city hospitals, where the sisters work as regular nurses without the "angel of mercy" sanctity surrounding nursing nuns in Catholic institutions. Not only are the nuns pleased with this arrangement, but the order finds it is economically more feasible. The nuns are paid a salary based on professional competence, and, moreover, they are exposed to the challenges of competitiveness with lay professionals.

Many hospitals formerly managed by Catholic orders are turning over the administration to lay boards, and some even are selling out their ownership. The nuns in Catholic hospitals today are hidden behind desks in most instances, and the patient rarely gets a chance to see any of them—except, of course, the very conspicuous sister in the cashier's window as he is being discharged. I think Catholic hospitals have hurt the image of true Christianity by their intransigence concerning payment of bills. Many people have been turned off completely by the high-handedness of a sister-cashier. The association of religion with money and power is never Christian, least of all when suffering is involved.

Nuns should work in hospitals, but I look forward to the day when the distinctly Catholic hospital fades from the scene. Nuns can give much better witness to Christ working shoulder to shoulder with their co-workers in the medical profession than as overlords in their own hospitals. I think nuns excel in the care of the sick and in medical research. After all, no one can gainsay the spirit of dedication and generosity of a person whose whole life is service to humanity. We expect a great deal from religious, and we usually get it if their circumstances and environment are favorable to a realistic involvement. I don't believe Catholic hospitals are the citadels of witness and mercy that they once were.

9. ARE YOU IN FAVOR OF THE CONFRATERNITY OF CHRISTIAN DOCTRINE?

§ NO

Most people will admit that the Confraternity, or CCD, has been more or less a failure. One of the reasons for this is the unstructured nature of the CCD. No one really knows what it is or what it is supposed to do. I have always considered CCD a rather inferior substitute for the Catholic school.

In my parish the CCD teacher is nothing but a stopgap. Very little cooperation or training is given him by the pastor of the parish, since he is not interested in the CCD in the first place. Why should he be? He has a very efficient and smoothly running school for the Catholic children. The only reason he has to run a CCD program is either because some parents do not want to send their children to Catholic schools or because the parish school is overcrowded.

The CCD has as its object the religious instruction and moral guidance of Catholic children in the public schools. The CCD meets once a week, and most of the teachers are patient volunteers who have to stand shotgun over an unruly and bored group of youngsters. In my parish the priest has to entice the kids to come to Christian doctrine classes, and then, after one hour of instruction, he allows them to use the gym for a dance. The volunteers have to stay around and chaperone the dance. Here again is another waste of manpower.

When people ask for the abolition of Catholic schools, I always smile. Let these intellectuals take over one CCD meeting and they will soon thank God for the nuns and brothers who staff our Catholic schools. The kids who are trained in the public schools are usually rowdy and disrespectful. They don't have to respect their public school teachers, because the principal stands firmly behind the rights of the child. I have heard of kids taunting their teachers, daring them to strike. Should the teacher raise a hand against them, the kids know they can have him dismissed and a law suit brought against the poor creature, who, generally, is only trying to do his job well.

If this attitude should appear in a religion classroom, there would be automatic chaos. This plus the need to pamper the children into coming to CCD creates an anarchistic situation. You will find that most parishes are phasing out the CCD, and that anyone who has had anything to do with the operation of the programs is sighing an enthusiastic "Amen."

❊ YES

People say that the CCD program is a substitute for a full religious education. But the CCD should be more than that. It is a substitute only to the person who thinks that the Catholic Church should own and staff its own schools. But once the errors in the privately owned school systems reveal themselves, then CCD emerges not as a substitute but as an essential program. Our experience with CCD has been anything but pleasant, but criticism of the program is with its operation rather than with its concept. The idea is a good one. What the program needs is expert and scientific implementation. Naturally, using untrained teachers to present a program whose major substance is dry and boring religious data does not represent a formula for success. But what is the concept of the CCD?

Rather than providing an entire educational program, the Church should concentrate on a realistic Christian education. Thus, the teacher, relieved of teaching algebra or Spanish, can spend time preparing interesting, innovative programs in which religion and the Christian message are invitingly presented. It means creating new responsibility for the parish, for it is the parish that is logically committed to the education of youth. Once it is no longer a stepchild of the Catholic school system, the CCD program can achieve not only its own identity but its implementation and maturity.

A group of nuns who specialized in the teaching of religion, which is known as catechetics, has set up shop in my parish. They have extended their influence beyond the classroom into the homes of the youngsters by visiting with the parents, checking on the background of the child to be instructed, and trying to strike up a healthy, casual relationship with the entire family. Teaching religion for them is not simply a one-hour-a-week or once-a-day chore. It is their life.

This small group of women has succeeded in reversing hostile attitudes toward the CCD. Youngsters look forward to religion courses at the Confraternity center, and parents know their children are receiving an in-depth training for life that touches on all phases of adult development. You can walk into a class there and find a trained nun teaching anything from music appreciation to guitar or ceramics. There is no Catholic school in the parish, but what the nuns have succeeded in doing through their wise and mature handling of religious education is something that no one will gainsay or criticize, particularly the pastor. Ask him if he wants a Catholic school and he'll say, "What for?"

Once parishes are reduced to a more realistic size, the role of the CCD center will be more effective, for CCD exists as a vehicle for providing meaningful and relevant communication between the Church and the family. Not only is it less financially oppressive than the present school system, but if skillfully handled, the CCD can augur a new day for Catholicism.

10. IS THERE A FUTURE FOR THE CATHOLIC SCHOOL SYSTEM?

§ YES

Stories are rampant today about the imminent demise of the parochial school system. I think that if we dismantle the school system, we'll strike a lethal blow at the Church itself, for it is in the schools that the kids learn about God. Isn't that just what the communists do when they take over a country—close the religious schools? They figure if they can take over the minds of the young, then they have a hold on tomorrow.

If one would take the time to read Pius XII's classical encyclical *Christian Education*, he would understand the importance the Church places on the proper schooling of the whole person. How can the Church expect to train its flock properly if it gives up its schools? In the United States the success of prominent Catholics is due in no small part to their parochial school education. If we abandon this citadel of truth, we abandon the future.

❈ NO

The Catholic school system has no future, because it no longer fills a real need in the Church. Ask any young person today who is a product of the parochial school system and he will tell you that he died of boredom in his religion classes. He looked for interest and meaning outside the Church, and found it in his transistor radio, in sit-ins, in peace marches. The Church has not been able to find the wavelength to tune in young people. Yet they continue to waste their time supporting the huge white elephants that are the Catholic schools.

Another reason for the impending demise of the school system is a simple case of mathematics. The present system is too costly, and the product does not warrant the investment. People are turning away from the Church, they are turning a deaf ear to pleas for money to support what they consider a dying system. Moreover, the quality of Catholic education cannot stand comparison with what the public schools, with government-financed programs, can offer.

I think that a better means of continuing Catholic education is through CCD catechetical centers, which more and more far-sighted parishes are adopting. If the parish is to become smaller, if finances dwindle, one need not be a clairvoyant to predict the number of days left to the once glorified Catholic school system.

X

SEX,
MARRIAGE,
AND
CENSORSHIP

To MOST PEOPLE four-letter words are indecent. Yet if we stop and think, most of the four-letter words have little, if any, meaning. They are simply blocks that people play with. You can use the word "intercourse," and it's quite acceptable. You can refer to a female dog as a bitch, and no one is offended. So why should four-letter words be shocking? People who often use such words in their daily conversations are horrified to hear them on TV or see them in print.

Should people be protected from sex? That's what censorship seems to imply. Isn't the Catholic Church the great defender of censorship? We have censorship in the movies, on the stage, in books, and it was only recently that the Church got rid of the Index of Forbidden Books.

What about birth control? Did you ever wonder why this is so evil? Birth control is perhaps the most controversial issue in the Church today. We are told that if you look long enough, you can find a priest who will tell you that birth control is no longer sinful. What do you think?

Divorce is explicitly condemned by Christ in the Gospel. But is the interpretation given to this text really valid? Did Christ really want an incompatible couple to go through living hell for the rest of their lives? Should the Church allow trial marriages? No one can make final vows in a religious order without going through at least four years of probation, yet couples are counseled against long engagements, and once they marry, they are bound together for life.

Have you ever dared to question your attitudes toward sex? Or have you simply accepted the Church's point of view without evaluating it? Sex is such a vital part of a person's life. If one is going to have to live intimately with something that is supposedly such a source of temptation and evil, then he owes it to himself to understand the why and wherefore of it all.

1. DO YOU NEED SEX?

§ NO

Sex is a necessary part of life, but it is a necessary evil. It is difficult to talk about it, and is embarrassing to many people. Some of man's biggest problems in keeping close to God arise from the stirrings of his sexual powers.

Sex is very important in marriage, but even husbands and wives have problems with it. Sexual acts are usually performed behind closed doors because of their salacious nature. If they were performed only for procreation, they would not be evil. Many movies today have explicit sex acts, and on Broadway there are plays that feature nude scenes. There is an overemphasis on sex in our society, and this emphasis is what is evil.

God gave us sexual organs for a purpose. But at the same time, he placed a strong obligation on us to experience restraint in the use of our sexual powers. It is this that most people overlook; the fact that sex means responsibility. I don't think the Catholic religion is against sex, as some would say. What the Church tries to emphasize is that the use of sex brings responsibility and therefore must be used wisely and in accord with its purpose.

Some people think that sex is nothing but pleasure and that's its purpose. Bodily enjoyment is all right, but man should aim for intellectual and spiritual pleasure rather than pure animal pleasure. A person who emphasizes sex and really needs it—is a slave to it—misses out on so much of life.

❊ YES

Naturally I need sex, with all that implies. My whole manner of living is conditioned by my sex. Sex is an appetite and a craving. I seek it through normal channels, and I don't like it to be made embarrassing. Sex is part of my being. God gave sex to mankind, and he made it deeply pleasurable.

If you regard sex in the abstract, it can be applied to animal, insect, or man. But since sex is so intertwined with the whole personality, to consider sex in the abstract is really impossible. The mistake of the Catholic religion has been to label sex evil or dangerous without justification. Naturally, if someone is a sex maniac or a pervert, then his use of sex is distorted. But that doesn't make sex dangerous.

Sex is exercised through a specific channel, as in marriage. Sex is an important part of marriage, not just for the purpose of having children, but for bringing two people into an enduring and fulfilling relationship. Through sex, two people can express their love, and increase it. If a person has a distorted view of sex before marriage, his chances of overcoming this and having a successful marriage are slim indeed.

We should go nude more often, for we will discover in our bodies the beauty of God's creation. Many people are afraid of looking at their bodies; they prefer to shroud themselves and make war on sex. They are unable to expand their minds to the totality of life. Of course, I realize that nudity is not the same as seductiveness. I don't advocate that. I just wish Catholicism would stop making everyone wear psychological fig leaves.

I need sex, and I feel I have learned to live with it; I recognize its power over me, and I accept it. In that way I am able to get on with the important task of living and assuming responsibility. I don't make my religion a game of hide-and-go-seek.

2. IS THE SIXTH COMMANDMENT THE GREATEST?

§ YES

Christ said that the greatest commandment was one of love, but our religion puts great emphasis on the Sixth and the Ninth Commandments, and with reason. Purity is pleasing to God. If you look at the way man lives, the way he washes and primps, how he likes everything nice and clean, you can understand how important these same qualities are to God. God wants his creatures to be pure and wholesome in his sight. Sins against the Sixth

Commandment—and those that are related, like masturbation, incest, and fornication—make us feel guilty and shameful. This is an indication of the value we place on purity. Many men would not marry a girl who is not a virgin. They feel that she has been defiled. And if she was so free before marriage, what assurance do they have that she won't have adulterous affairs after marriage?

Christ himself put much emphasis on purity. He never married, and his Church insists on a celibate clergy. Little children are pure and clean in the sight of God. Christ told us to become as little children, and he gave us the sacrament of penance so that we might never be forced to live with the stain of impurity on our soul.

I worry a great deal about keeping the Sixth Commandment. Temptations are more soul-shattering today than ever before. I pray daily, make many sacrifices, and often fast, because this evil is so hard to get rid of. Christ wants us to love, but love can be found only in a pure person.

✳ *NO*

The greatest commandment is love; this is what the Church teaches us. It is difficult to understand, however, how love can be the object of a law and a commandment. I don't think you can force someone to love. The Sixth Commandment is rather pointless. All it says is that we shouldn't commit adultery. Perhaps the ancient Hebrews needed such an imperative statement. But I don't. If I am married and truly in love, I will not be tempted to commit adultery.

I cannot see how the Church can conclude from the one commandment forbidding adultery that therefore a hundred and one other acts are also forbidden, such as fornication, incest, masturbation, and so on. Psychologists are almost unanimous in stating that most of the marriage problems in our day are born of guilt over supposed offenses against the Sixth Commandment. If Catholics were as careful to avoid hurting their neighbor, stealing, and backbiting as they are to avoid sins against purity, their religion would be more virile and certainly more effective.

Undue stress on the Sixth Commandment produces moral

eunuchs. I don't say that adultery is to be advocated. I just say that the emphasis on this commandment is most distressing. I think Catholics need a revised theology of sex that is sane. As it stands now, the rest of the world is getting involved in waging war against war, poverty, and the deprivation of human dignity. Instead of nursing their phobias and psychological immaturities caused by coping with the Sixth Commandment, Catholics too should be promulgating the concepts of love and brotherhood bequeathed to them by the risen Saviour. The ugly thing about the Sixth Commandment is that in crushing sex it diminishes the person.

3. IS BIRTH CONTROL EVIL?

§ YES

Birth control is a mortal sin. It always has been and always will be. People are suffering the pains of eternal fire because they flew in the face of the Creator by usurping his power of life and death over the unborn. I like the saying of a priest who always tells those who advocate birth control that they are one generation too late. God in his goodness has allowed man to share with him in the power of creation. To me this is an awesome privilege and responsibility. That a person should, through selfishness and personal greed, thwart the purpose of creation is a most heinous insult to the God of love.

If one asks himself what is the primary purpose of marriage, he will recall that its purpose is the procreation of children. "Increase and multiply" was Christ's command. For someone to use the sacred sacrament of matrimony merely as an altar for his own pleasure is a sacrilege. The sexual organs are designed for producing life. The man complements the woman, and vice versa. To use these organs for sheer pleasure alone is to violate nature.

People who practice birth control are selfish. When they are old and want to enjoy the twilight years of their lives, the sins of their youth will be visited on them, for no one will want to be with them. They will have no children, no one to continue their life's work, and other people will be too busy with their own lives to worry about them.

The Church allows the rhythm method of birth control. Pope Paul is right not to reverse his position on the natural law and allow birth control under any other form. I take a pill to ease a headache, but I don't believe in taking pills to avoid life and maturity. Those who upset the laws of nature are bound to find that nature will exact its toll, just as a person who flouts the law of gravity will soon discover the inexorability of this law.

✳ NO

I don't think that birth control of itself is evil. I am against all moralizing that is predicated on an abstract concept; in this case, natural law. The control of births is sometimes necessary because of terrible population problems, such as those in India, China, and Latin America. It is very easy for Pope Paul to visit India or South America and promise the people eternal salvation, but what they need right now is food and dignity. His refusal to accept theological and medical investigations advocating birth control is indeed incomprehensible.

I think the Church's position that birth control violates natural law is ridiculous. No one really knows what natural law is anyway. God gave us sex with responsibility. The Catholic Church makes a big issue out of birth control. It seems to be the unforgivable sin. In the confessional priests will harangue an individual who practices birth control. Yet some of these priests don't have a clue about the suffering and anguish involved in bringing up and providing for a family. To the celibate, abstinence is the only answer to overpopulation and economic hardship. But he himself has no idea of how important the sex act is to personality development and the maturation of married love. He will advise twin beds, then close the door of his box to shut out the broken hearts and coarse realities. Priests practice birth control in celibacy, and nature has its own way of striking a balance between population and overpopulation.

I think we should advocate birth control for the reason that it is not wrong in itself. The biblical text describing the sin of

Onan is spurious. The interpretation given by Augustine, and those following him, to this text is a masterful deception and distortion. Let's not make an issue of birth control.

4. SHOULD THE CHURCH ALLOW DIVORCE?

§   NO

Divorce is one evil that the Catholic Church cannot reverse itself on. This practice was condemned by Christ himself in the Gospels. Divorce, moreover, attacks the very fabric of the family, and makes a mockery of the sacramental character of matrimony. We know all too well the evils of divorce, the broken homes, the abandoned children. Divorce makes marriage into a parlor game. It destroys the important Christian qualities of courage and endurance. Once a person has an argument or he gets tired of his family life, there is nothing to stop him from dropping all his responsibilities.

I know many people who suffer untold pain and anguish because one mistake caused them to abandon a beautiful family relationship. The husband is allowed to visit the children only on certain occasions, and he loses the depth and richness of genuine family life. In return, he has nothing but emptiness and pain. Who can ever understand the loneliness and alienation that divorce leaves in its wake? The unhappy lives of divorced people should be enough to convince us that divorce is a definite evil.

If there is one thing that the Catholic Church has shown, it is that the family is the bedrock of society. The Church protects and guides the family in many ways, lest the destruction of the family spell the dissolution of society. The popes have always taught us that the family is the basic unit of society. Once the family goes, what do we have left but a chaotic and selfish civilization? Rome fell because of this, and so have other once-powerful civilizations. For the Church to allow divorce would be to sanction the disintegration of religion itself. What God has joined together, let no man put asunder.

✻ YES

I think Catholics have an inherited fear of divorce. We would much rather see two people going through hell and black despair than allow them to separate and find another partner. I think this all stems from our masochistic background. The Catholic religion is predicated on pain and suffering in this life, so long as it is the other fellow who is doing the suffering. When marital discord touches the lives of those who have money, they are miraculously able to have their indissoluble unions dissolved. But those who have a slim bank account must accept dishonor and excommunication.

Our treatment of marriage is unreal and un-Christian. When Christ spoke of divorce, he was not insisting that people go through hell for the rest of their lives. I think you have to take what a man says in the context of his own teachings and his own gentleness. Such a harsh and unyielding position is out of character for Christ. He was not vindictive.

I believe that the Church should be mature enough to recognize that a person can make a mistake in marriage as in anything else. If Christ instituted the sacrament of penance to give a person a second chance, then I think he also meant this for marriage. I know there are difficulties involved, but they are not insuperable. The family will be better preserved through love and understanding, not harsh, unyielding regulations. People who are not allowed to separate usually do anyway, and because they are treated like heretics they turn bitter. Their loss, I believe, is more real than the feigned loss of "family."

5. SHOULD THE CHURCH BE SO FIRM AGAINST HOMOSEXUALS?

§ YES

St. Paul in his Epistle to the Romans refers to homosexuality as an abomination. It is a perversion wherein the nadir of lust and lewdness is reached. In the Old Testament, homosexuals were considered the chaff of society and their activities were made the object of derision and disdain. Today, we find more and more people turning in this direction. The hairstyles and the foppery currently in vogue can only lead to ambivalence on the part of our young people. It is the role of the Church to cry against this prostitution of morality.

English law considers homosexual relations between consenting adults as tolerable, as does the state of Illinois. The cinema of late is treating the problem openly; for example, in "Thérèse and Isabel" lesbianism is the theme. A play on Broadway hides nothing and wrestles frankly with the problem. Our society is becoming more and more aware of the existence of homosexuality, and this is the inherent danger. The media tend to glorify those who engage in this practice. We hear the sophisticated commentators on late-night talk shows hinting rather brazenly that homosexuality is not really as horrid as was once thought. There was a time when such ideas were not mentioned in polite company. Today the thrust is to shock, and so engage listeners. It has reached the point where one begins to wonder what our moral index is. We can be happy that the Church has ever remained faithful to its role as guardian of the morals of the people of God.

Homosexuality is patently contrary to nature. Man is ordained to live with women. His anatomy is constructed to complement a woman's. So too do man and woman complement each other psychologically and intellectually. Men who act or dress like women are sick, and they need help, not adulation and imitation. Those who persist in attempting to change the moral climate of our nation do so from questionable motives. To foist a sick practice on young people and sit back while they experiment and endanger their future merits nothing less than severe censure and sheer disgust. The glorious Greek and Roman civilizations fell because men became fops and were too weak to defend their frontiers.

We are witnessing a dangerous trend and a breakdown in morals. Do you wonder why the Catholic Church is so unforgiving when the future of the world is at stake?

✳ *NO*

Homosexuality is a moral problem, to be sure. But just as I don't feel the state, through its police, should have any control over the aberrations of individuals so long as they do not hurt anyone else, so too I don't feel it is the role of the Church to judge any man. I think that in the case of homosexuality, the Church forgets Christ's admonition to "hate the sin and love the sinner." Homosexuality violates the Sixth Commandment, and, in the interest of "saving the sinner," I have heard of priests treating homosexuals as if they were rapists or murderers. Charity, justice, and kindness disappear when the Church is confronted with homosexuality. And it is for this reason that I believe the Church overreacts in these instances.

I do not hear the Church speak out as forcefully when children are seriously threatened by disease, racism, and hunger. I do not hear the Church at all when gross militancy is substituted for patriotism, or when sincere Catholics are treated like dirt by some of its functionaries. But when homosexuality is mentioned, the collective back of officialdom seems to arch and the Church spews fire and brimstone.

When it comes to the exercise of freedom, the Church does not come across well. Many clergy look down their nose at the young people who wear long hair, who experiment with pot, or who practice homosexuality. These people are ostracized, and yet at no time do they have a more urgent need for the help and understanding of the Church.

Homosexuality is a private affair in the truest sense of the word. If two people are not hurting anyone, I don't see why I must abandon basic civility and charity in my dealings with them. Although I don't agree with what they are doing, that does not mean I should judge and condemn them. I have the same attitude toward masturbation. I don't agree that masturbation is any sort of answer to life's problems, but many young people do masturbate. The Church has to learn that it cannot control the lives of men. Its role in the world is to inspire through example, not to dictate through sword rattling and excommunication.

I think of the example of Christ with the woman taken in adultery. I am sure he did not condone her actions, but yet he understood her and could sense the frustration that drove her to infidelity. He was not patronizing, and he did not try to change her mind. He was just there, understanding and kind. If the Church were to try this method, I am sure we all would fear the future less.

6. DO YOU APPROVE OF SEX EDUCATION IN THE SCHOOLS?

§ NO

The Catholic Church has been outspoken in its disapproval toward the teaching of sex in schools. Elaborate instruction in matters about sex helps no one, especially impressionable young people. Furthermore, such physical explanations are inadequate. They do not furnish the safeguards and cautions so necessary if one is to educate his children to the proper understanding of the virtue of purity. Sex education in the schools is morally harmful, because it inflames the very curiosity it is supposed to quench.

Sex education is predicated on the belief that knowledge of sex educates the child to his responsibilities. But how can public school teachers, who themselves are so often devoid of morals and religion, give the child a virtuous attitude toward sex? What we end up with in sex-education courses is the teacher telling the child how to take precautions against disease. If these classes are mixed, as is often the case, the danger is that the child will do some extracurricular homework to test the theories of the teacher.

The attitude of the Catholic Church in sex matters is to display a Christian reticence. Some people say that to the pure, all things are pure. But when St. Paul used this text, he was not referring to sex, but to the use of unclean animals under the obsolete Jewish law. Whenever you publicly discuss sex, especially among young people, you destroy modesty and shame. These are the natural protectors of chastity.

Where should sex education take place? I believe it is best

taught in the home, under the guidance of a loving father and a virtuous mother. The priest also can give sexual instruction, for he studied these matters in detail in the seminary in order to guide people in this most serious and most volatile area. As a physician of the soul, the priest is responsible for instilling the proper respect and obedience toward the laws of God on sex. Let's not turn our classrooms into arenas of license and promiscuity, leaving to strangers the all-important task of forming our children.

❋ YES

The home is the ideal place for the teaching of sex, but most parents are not equal to the task. The average Catholic parent would not know how to treat the physical side of sex, simply because he himself did not receive the proper training as a youngster. Most people picked up their knowledge of sex from other youngsters or in the gutter. It is unusual to find a parent today, especially a Catholic parent, who is balanced and open in his attitude toward sex. Consequently, education is best left to professionals within the school.

Because the Catholic Church is so prudish with regard to sex, it hates the idea of letting non-Catholics instruct in this delicate area. It fears that the public school teacher will fill the youngster's head with all sorts of immoral suggestions, hinting that there is nothing wrong with masturbation, or petting, or premarital sex.

Sex education is a very specialized and technical field. The people in charge of sex education are professionals, and the programs, based on careful research, are sensitive to the need for sound ethics and morals. The teachers are acutely aware of the problems of the civilization we live in, and they strive to uplift the young and help them toward maturity, not lead them into immorality.

The Catholic Church confuses sex education with sensuality. Its opposition to sex education in the schools stems from a basic lack of confidence in science and in public education. Young people learn about sex earlier now through television and other media, so, more than ever, professional competence must be brought to bear on the problem of inadequate sex education. In what better way can the Church bring about proper and balanced attitudes than to support the professional programs in the schools?

7. SHOULD THE CHURCH ABANDON CENSORSHIP?

§ NO

Many people think that "censorship" is a dirty word. They curl up their lips and frown when they hear it. Yet all of us practice some type of censorship in our own lives and over those we love. We keep poison away from our children. Isn't that a form of censorship? We make our children wear warm clothing in winter. Isn't that telling them what to do? We spare no effort to keep our loved ones from harm's path. Censorship is a form of control, and is exercised to protect others.

The Church has the responsibility toward all of its children to make sure that they are not hurt, or stopped on their pilgrimage to paradise. Not everyone in the world is our friend, and not everyone wants us to get to heaven.

Many people care about nothing except making money and more money. They specialize in putting out filth, obscene books and magazines and movies. The Church steps in and tells us that we should avoid these evil materials. It puts up warning signals saying: Stop, look, and listen before you go there or buy that. We have warning labels on our cigarette packs now. Why do we complain when the Church warns us that a book or movie is potentially dangerous to our eternal salvation?

Censorship is necessary to protect us from the flow of filth and garbage that constantly invades our everyday lives. Rather than screaming so loudly about censorship, we should be grateful that the Church alerts us to the occasions of sin.

✳ YES

Censorship is predicated on the belief that the individual is neither intelligent enough nor mature enough to evaluate a situation properly. Some people speciously compare censorship to protective labeling. I am all for warnings in situations where I am not equipped to make an evaluation. But most people are mature enough to recognize the dangers that face them in life. Censorship is an infringement on freedom.

Surely we must realize that censorship is based on specific canons or guidelines. What makes a censor more capable than I am to evaluate a particular item? What certitude do I have that his guidelines are objective and not simply his pet peeves? How do I know that he is not foisting his own sexual problems on me? No two people are the same. No two people react to a given situation in the same way. Censorship is predicated on the principle that we are all made the same way. Physically this is not true; it is even less true psychologically and morally. We all come from different backgrounds, and we all react differently.

The Legion of Decency always annoyed me. I have been told that its censorship board was made up of ladies and priests. How these people could assume that I would react to a film in the same way they did, or how they could dare to prophesy a uniform reaction, was an enigma to me. Who censors the censor? No one is infallible, and no one can tell me that the censors themselves were not sensitive and prudish. If they found a particular scene provocative, perhaps the reasons lay hidden in their own psyches. Perhaps they hadn't lived and read enough. The Church should not treat us as children.

8. IS VIRGINITY MORE PERFECT THAN MARRIAGE?

§ YES

Virginity is highly prized in the Church, because it was the state embraced by Jesus Christ and his mother Mary. Marriage is basically a concession to man's lower nature. The sacrament of matrimony elevates man's instinct above that of the animals, and places the sex instinct within the proper context of the family. The Church also extols virginity in its priests; celibacy is considered more perfect than marriage. In the Old Testament a man who had intercourse with a woman was considered unclean, and he could not perform any rites within the temple without a waiting period. The Church never looks down upon marriage, but it prefers virginity. In heaven, where perfection is the common state, humans are not given in marriage. Virginity is considered a perfection because it is one of the evangelical counsels, something one doesn't have to do but which he does in order to imitate Christ more perfectly.

Virginity, then, is the summit of self-denial and the total rejection of the flesh and the world. This is its attraction. Virginity symbolizes the pure love of God, which ultimately transcends the world. In virginity we see the eschatological dimension of the Church: ultimate self-denial reaches out in hope. We do not claim that sexual abstinence is in itself a virtue. On the contrary, it is a neutral state and not actively opposed to concupiscence.

What makes virginity important is that Christ, through his own virginity, made it an ideal. He did not impose it on everyone, but said that anyone who could follow his example should do so. Virginity must not be a mere outward sign, because then its witness to Christ could be destroyed by ambition, power, even by prudery or a basic resentment against life. In other words, virginity has a value only inasmuch as we are following the example of Christ in its totality.

❋ NO

Marriage and virginity are not conceptually opposed, as though one were more perfect than the other. Virginity has its place and so does marriage. In its overemphasis on virginity, the Church has made marriage seem something imperfect. Marriage is a sacrament, a sign of the union existing between Christ and his Church. The Church has made extensive use of the rich allegorical implications of marriage to explain its own concept of itself and its apostolate. The Old and New Testaments abound in such allegory.

St. Paul tells us that it is better to marry than to burn, by which he meant that marriage and virginity are distinct vocations, and that it is within the competence of the individual to make the choice that he thinks best expresses his role in the kingdom of God. Through the sacrament of matrimony, married couples participate in a special way in the saving mystery of Christ and the Church, and, in fact, through marriage God's own covenant with man is made visible. Marriage has a prophetic function within the world, and in the family the sanctity of marriage is realized.

The world would benefit greatly if the Church would abolish this artificial opposition between marriage and virginity. Moreover, people should understand that the sex instinct is part of the total picture of marriage, and if marriage is honorable and prophetic, sex itself assumes a nobility. Rather than thinking of marriage as a device to justify sex, we would see marriage as an expression of a love that unites two people in a common response to the love of God.

9. IS CHURCH APPROVAL OF ABORTION A POSSIBILITY?

§ NO

Abortion is murder, and can never be justified. I speak now of deliberate abortion, and I am not considering the principle of the double effect, as when a fetus is removed during surgery performed to save the mother's life. Abortion is increasing in the United States, as more and more people are rejecting traditional attitudes. Some priests even maintain that a fetus is not human. But they forget that man is in a constant state of biological change until the moment of death, when his whole being achieves its fulfillment in God. Birth is only a beginning.

Abortion, defined as the interruption of a pregnancy before the fetus is viable, is a direct attack on innocent life. The law of

God and the law of nature are violated; we are all held to obey the Fifth Commandment: THOU SHALT NOT KILL. The lives of both the mother and the child are equally sacred, and not even the state can authorize a murder. God is the source of life, and he alone has the power to take it away. Abortion is a dreadful evil, and leads one to suspect the moral caliber of those advocating such a cruel slaughter of innocent lives.

The Catholic Church is firm in its belief in the sacredness of life. It never forces anyone to be a Catholic or to remain a Catholic. If the question of abortion were not a moral issue, the Church would not be so adamant in its position. It allows its members freedom of thought and expression at all times. Everyone knows that there is a wide spectrum of opinion among Catholics on many questions in philosophy, theology, psychiatry, and other sciences. But in a situation that is obviously prohibited by divine law, Catholics have to submit to the Church, for it speaks as Christ in fulfillment of its divine mandate to teach all nations.

✳ YES

The so-called evil of abortion rests on the premise that human life is present in the fetal stage. Today modern science denies this, as does civil law. We should not be surprised at such a position, since St. Thomas Aquinas himself once rejected the concept of fetal life, and as a consequence rejected the Immaculate Conception. Since abortion hinges on a biological question, one must look to biology and not theology for the resolution of the problem. One must not close his mind to science. Such a closed attitude could result in the Church finding itself in a ridiculous position whereby its prestige and the value of the moral law itself would suffer.

What happens when the Church pulls the lid down on moral issues based on biological and psychological premises? Look at the current furor that Pope Paul's anti-birth control resolution has brought on. The real problem has become a problem of authority. The Church finds itself saying, "This is such and such because I say so." Thinking men walk away from this kind of authoritarianism, and a turbulent crisis in authority results. The Church is right in saying that nature tells man not to kill. But the Church has supported wars and, many times, unjust wars. It explains this away by finding extenuating circumstances—which make a mockery of the moral leadership the Church claims.

Everyone realizes that a fetus is not a person. This is obvious from the very nature of gestation. When life enters the fetus and when fetal life becomes human life are debatable questions. How can the Church be dogmatic, then, in an area that is itself so positively undefined?

10. IS PREMARITAL SEX WRONG?

§ YES

The primary purpose of marriage is the perfection of husband and wife in mutual love and devotion, and also the procreation of children. Those who indulge in premarital sex run the serious risk of bringing children into the world without the proper family context within which to safeguard their rights. Premarital sex is basically selfish. The couple satisfy their desire for pleasure without assuming the responsibility inherent in intercourse. The Church is most understanding and sympathetic about the problems of engaged couples, and it discourages long engagements because it knows these are morally inflammable and real occasions of sin. Were the Church to permit the promiscuity implied in premarital relationships, it would be striking at the very heart of the family.

Sex is supposed to be an expression of love and respect, but always within the sacramental context. Once sex is used simply to satisfy desire, then it becomes defiled. Young people today delude themselves into believing that sexual promiscuity is indifferent, but their attitude stems from an adolescent inability to look to the consequences of their actions and to relate these acts to a more universal picture. The advocates of free love do not realize that their permissiveness opens up avenues of escape for teenagers, many of whom are psychologically unable to cope with the emotional aspect of sex and become permanently injured as persons. Teen-agers cause untold grief to their families, and young boys bring undue hardship into the lives of girls they "play around with." Educators are unhappy about the number of unwed mothers, and recognize in this phenomenon a general breakdown in the moral fiber of the nation. It is their task to make young people understand why free love and promiscuity corrode the basic unit of society, the family.

✳ NO

I don't see anything wrong with premarital sex. In fact, I think the act of intercourse is one of the highest tributes that a man can pay to a woman, and, given the proper motivation, it cannot be other than an expression of love. I am not thinking of sex performed in the back seats of cars, of sex as found in brothels or stag films. I mean two people who are very much in love and who plan to marry. Since by their engagement they have committed themselves to one another, it is understandable that they would want to express that commitment through sexual intercourse. To forbid them this is not only cruel, but it indicates a lack of understanding of the basic biological and psychological needs of human beings.

Two people should not put a ceiling on their expression of love, stating that they will limit their love to kissing or nervous embracing. Love has no limits, and neither does the expression of love. If it should lead to sexual intercourse, what evil has been done? These are people who are going to get married and have already given themselves to one another. The Church is unrealistic when it treats sex merely as a biological issue. Persons who are committed to one another must grow during their engagement period, and their love must also mature. The rare and precious moments spent in complete union serve to deepen and enlarge their consciousness of one another, and help to develop a relationship that is sacred.

Respect, loyalty, understanding, and mutual support develop in a proper and respectful use of premarital sex. The question of pregnancy is easily solved by use of the pill or other contraceptive measures. Of course, this is a decision that must be left to the conscience of the persons involved.

CONCLUSION

WHERE DO WE GO FROM HERE?

THE PURPOSE IN writing this book was to delight and to irritate, but more specifically, to prod the reader to think about the issues involved in a renewed Church. Whether or not our purpose was achieved is difficult to assess. But we hope that the least that can be said is that the book was interesting, for we tried to present both points of view on vexing questions. We tried simply to present the issues.

Now that you have read both points of view, the rest is up to you. The only one that can do anything about yourself is you. You can fight, or switch. But only you can do it.

We honestly hope you will stay with the Catholic Church, and help it through these trying days. If everyone walks out, then who will help to renew? It is understandable that you might feel a bit alone and dejected once you realize that the Church is not going to come out and give dogmatic answers to basic issues any more. But heaven only knows what a challenge this reality is.

We think you should address yourself to the challenge. But to do this correctly and wisely, you will have to accept some basic facts of religious life.

First of all, you must not look back, either in anger or in nostalgia. Yesterday is gone. Change is a reality in your religion. You must not put your hand to the plow and then look back on the good old days. That will reduce you either to inertia or despair. Those who think that the Catholic Church is going to return to the posture of yesterday are deluding themselves and wasting valuable time. They are sighing after the wind.

Secondly, you must keep informed. You may have already chosen one position to the exclusion of others. You may have found yourself more a realist than an idealist. Or vice versa. But nonetheless, you must have caught the message that powerful change is sweeping through the Church. Unless you bridge the communication and information gap in your life, you will be living in another world. Information on the changing Church is available in our current religious literature. Attend parish meetings and demand to know what is going on. Sooner or later, if enough people band together, information will be forthcoming.

Finally, accept your new relationship to the Church and to God. The accent today is on personal responsibility. The Church makes fewer demands—but expects so much more. The Lenten regulations are gone. Some say Sunday Mass will be optional. What the Church is saying is simply this: Look, I can't force you to relate to God in any given way. Why don't you find God and let your response to his love be the guiding force in your life?

Exciting? Thrilling? Yes, every bit of it. But it demands a responsible use of freedom.

You can reject all this advice. But then, you will have to accept the consequences. The rate of change is powerful. It makes one dizzy. You can say, I will not change. But then your renewed Church will be leaving you behind. You will be setting out on your own. Your psychological balance could be threatened. Your security will be gone. And you will soon find yourself all alone. Choose instead to be a forceful influence in the world of today. Choose to be a temple of the living word. And dare to speak and live it.